Our Debt to Greece and Rome

EDITORS

GEORGE DEPUE HADZSITS, PH.D.

DAVID MOORE ROBINSON, PH.D., LL.D.

MARTIAL

AND

THE MODERN EPIGRAM

BY

PAUL NIXON

COOPER SQUARE PUBLISHERS, INC.

NEW YORK

1963

Published 1963 by Cooper Square Publishers, Inc.
59 Fourth Avenue, New York 3, N.Y.
Library of Congress Catalog Card No. 63-10304

To

KENNETH CHARLES MORTON SILLS

PRESIDENT OF BOWDOIN COLLEGE

ADMIRED EXECUTIVE AND CHERISHED FRIEND

CONTENTS

[vii]

MARTIAL

AND

THE MODERN EPIGRAM

MARTIAL
AND THE
MODERN EPIGRAM

I. THE EPIGRAM

OFTEN it is the most common thing that is most difficult to define. One is not obliged to marry and rear a family in order to make this inglorious discovery, but that is one way to make it. Our domestic definition of a dodo may be less successful than our definition of. shoes or ships or sealing wax, yet it is apt to be distinctly more successful than our definition of life, or of love, or of a hundred other familiar mysteries.

Macaulay describes Atterbury's defense of the letters of Phalaris as " the best book ever written by any man on the wrong side of a question of which the writer was profoundly ignorant." Madame de Staël observes: " The more I see of men, the better I like dogs." La Rochefoucauld remarks: " All of us have sufficient fortitude to endure the misfortunes of others." Much prose literature, we perceive, from Herodotus to Wells, is lightened, or obscured, by similar verbal flashes, sudden, short, devastating, and we who are not devastated, or at least those of us who do not insist that all the writers we value shall at all times see life steadily and see it whole, generally view such coruscations without dismay.

Now despite La Monnoie's protest that an epigram in prose is a cavalryman dismounted, most of us contentedly regard these pointed, antithetical sayings as epigrams, prose epigrams. Yet we somehow persist in thinking of an epigram as being primarily and preferably a poem, and, if we had to describe it somewhat particularly without having an opportunity to take the matter under consideration — and to consult an encyclopaedia — we should be apt to state that it was a short poem ending with a playful or vicious thrust at somebody or something. Possibly, among our pleasing memories of things forgot, there lingers a faint recollection of Boileau's curt definition, "a *bon mot* set off with a couple of rhymes," or of some descriptive verse like that of William Walsh:

[4]

An epigram should be — if right —
Short, simple, pointed, keen, and bright,
   A lively little thing!
Like wasp with taper body — bound
By lines — not many, neat and round,
   All ending in a sting.

At any rate, such recollections seem to approve
our unstudied definition, and we are willing to
let it stand, unless our auditors protest. But
if they do protest and we feel forced to investi-
gate, we rather regretfully learn that it is not
so simple.

No, not for the wealth of all those that despise thee,
Though that would make Europe's whole opulence
   mine.

In what respect are these lines, from an attack
upon the Prince Regent for his treatment of
Sheridan, less an epigram than Landor's disposition of the Georges,

   George the First was always reckoned
   Vile — but viler George the Second;
   And what mortal ever heard
   Any good of George the Third?
   When from earth the Fourth descended,
   God be praised, the Georges ended,

[5]

or than Samuel Johnson's more subtle dises-
teem of one of the same monarchs,

> *Augustus still survives in Maro's strain,*
> *And Spenser's verse prolongs Eliza's reign;*
> *Great George's acts let tuneful Cibber sing,*
> *For Nature form'd the Poet for the King?*

This is the easiest of the questions which
begin to obtrude themselves as we try to read
our way, first through modern English epigrams, to a satisfactory definition. We find it
reasonably answered in Coleridge's distich:

> *What is an epigram? A dwarfish whole,*
> *Its body brevity, and wit its soul.*

Then what of the numerous epigrammatic passages in such poems as *The Rape of the Lock*
and *Don Juan* which are entirely complete in
themselves? Why not call the *Dunciad* or
Hudibras a garland of epigrams? No doubt
we could, were these poems literally nothing
but a succession of " dwarfish wholes." Yet
what of this very dwarfishness? We find that
Chesterfield's epigram, *On Mr. Nash's Picture
at Full Length, between the Busts of Sir Isaac
Newton and Mr. Pope, at Bath,* consists of

twenty-four lines, without including the title; that Francis Thynne's "epigram," *The Courte and Countrey*, drags its slow length along for one hundred and twelve lines; that Jonson's "epigram," *On the Famous Voyage*, contains one hundred and ninety-six lines. The quaint classifications in Knox's *Elegant Extracts* — "Epic and Miscellaneous"; "Epigrams, Epitaphs and other Little Pieces"; "Songs, Ballads, &c. &c." — where we see Goldsmith's very ample *Retaliation* grouped with Dr. Aldrich's *Five Reasons for Drinking*,

> Good wine; a friend; or being dry;
> Or lest we should be by and by;
> Or, any other reason why,

begin to seem not so ridiculously helpless, after all. When is an epigram too long to be an epigram — or, for that matter, too short? Is it merely because of excessive length that Peter Pindar's *The Pilgrims and the Peas* and Somerville's *The Officious Messenger* are called Tales, not Epigrams? They end, eventually, with a point.

Lines "neat and round," says Walsh. Or, as George Birdseye phrases it,

> *The diamond's virtues well might grace*
> *The epigram, and both excel*
> *In brilliancy in smallest space,*
> *And power to cut, as well.*

How essential is this brilliance? How rigorously must we insist upon that " exquisite polish of form and diction " which so often is declared to be, and so often seems to be, the very stuff of the epigram? Burns' quatrain on *Commissary Goldie's Brains*,

> *Lord, to account who dares thee call,*
> *Or e'er dispute thy pleasure?*
> *Else why within so thick a wall*
> *Enclose so poor a treasure?*

is certainly an epigram by all the rules we know. But is

> *In se'enteen hunder an' forty-nine,*
> *The deil gat stuff to mak a swine,*
> *An' cuist it in a corner;*
> *But by and by he changed his plan,*
> *An' made it something like a man,*
> *An' ca'd it Andrew Turner,*

too rude and slovenly to deserve the title? If so, what are we to call it? If not, how far are

[8]

we to go toward designating as epigrams the satirical verse in *Punch* or *Life*, the whimsies of Gelett Burgess and the Herfords, even the Limericks and the other amusing metrical trifles of our newspaper columnists, when they end with a sting? What shall we call the many little squibs of the Hood and Hook type whose effect is so entirely dependent on pun or word play, like Burns' *The Kirk of Lamington*,

> As *cauld a wind as ever blew,*
> A *caulder kirk, and in't but few;*
> A *caulder preacher never spak;* —
> Ye'*se a' be het ere I come back,*

or worse, like Dr. Donne's distich,

> I *am unable, yonder begger cries,*
> To *stand or move; if he say true, hee lies,*

or worst, like Hook's familiar impromptu,

> Here *comes Mr. Wynter, surveyor of taxes,*
> I *advise you to give him whatever he axes,*
> And *that, too, without any nonsense or flummery,*
> For *though his name's Wynter, his actions are summary?*

Dismissing for the time our questions regarding the epigram's brevity and polish, two of our tentative triad of qualities, let us consider the third, its sting.

> Freind, for your Epitaphs I'm grieved,
>> Where still so much is said,
> One half will never be believed,
>> The other never read.

This quatrain of Pope's is obviously an epigram — brevity, polish, sting, all are there. But what has become of this third element in his,

> Nature and Nature's laws lay hid in night:
> God said, " Let Newton be! " and all was light,

or in his splendid epitaphs, such as those on Mrs. Corbet and on Kneller? We find that Jonson's *Book of Epigrams,* which he terms the " ripest " of his studies, contains not only many mordant jests, but also many noble epitaphs and eulogies of members of the " tribe of Ben." Burns wrote:

> Light lay the earth on Billy's breast,
>> His chicken heart so tender:
> But build a castle on his head,
>> His skull will prop it under;

He also wrote, on Robert Aiken:

> *Know thou, O stranger to the fame*
> *Of this much lov'd, much honour'd name,*
> *(For none that knew him need be told)*
> *A warmer heart death ne'er made cold,*

calling them both "epitaphs." It soon becomes apparent that our greatest English epigrammatists have almost always regarded the epitaph, and have very often regarded its companion piece, the eulogy, as being but varieties of the epigram, varieties in which brevity and polish generally remain, while the final sting gives place to something else, frequently to pointed praise.

But we shortly learn that it is not only the epitaph and eulogy which seem to be epigrams without the sting. From John Heath's,

> *In Beatrice did all perfections grow,*
> *That she could wish or Nature could bestow.*
> *When Death, enamour'd with that excellence,*
> *Straight grew in love with her and took her hence,*

to William Watson's,

> *She dwelt among us till the flowers, 'tis said,*
> *Grew jealous of her; with precipitate feet,*
> *As loth to wrong them unawares, she fled.*
> *Earth is less fragrant now, and heaven more*
> *sweet,*

[11]

we come upon countless brief and tender elegies, closing with some poignant cry, some fond fancy, which have led their writers and their readers, both, to call them epigrams. And from Thomas Campion to Austin Dobson we discover countless little love poems ending with some gay vagary, some delicate conceit, pretty trifles like *The White Rose*, sent by a Yorkist gentleman to his Lancastrian mistress,

> *If this fair rose offend thy sight,*
> *Placed in thy bosom bare,*
> *'Twill blush to find itself less white,*
> *And turn Lancastrian there,*

deft rhapsodies, blithe plaints, where the tone is so light, the point so patent, as to make us yield still more ground and admit that perhaps they, too, are rightly classed as epigrams. The further we read, the worse our definition fares. We meet with more and more stingless epigrams. In content, collectively, they embrace almost all creation, and the Creator, also. In form, they often have not even that final, unmistakable point that we thought essential. We become so bewildered that it is a real relief to find traces of bewilderment elsewhere, to find, for instance, that a Palgrave includes a

Lylye's *Cupid and Campaspe,* or a Jonson's *Drink to me only with thine eyes,* in his collection of songs and lyrics with quite as much assurance as a Dodd includes them in his collection of epigrams. It is at least clear to us, however, that either the definition with which we began is distressingly meagre, or that many eminent modern epigrammatists have been widely mistaken in their terminology.

If, in our confusion, we consult the critics, we learn that this matter of the epigram's " sting " is one of those Serbonian bogs of letters upon both sides of which high and reverend authorities lift up their heads. One group profess to be supported by the *Greek Anthology,* that collection of " some four thousand epigrams by some three hundred writers of some seventeen centuries of Greek literature; " the other group profess to be upheld by " Martial and most modern epigrammatists." The extremists on one side inform us that the simplicity, liveliness, and point of the real epigram, exemplified in the *Anthology,* have been debauched into coarseness, personality, and sting in the counterfeit epigram, that of Martial and his successors, whose verses are nothing but "satires in brief," "ephemeral lampoons." The extremists on the other side assure us that the *Epigramme à la Grecque* is feeble, flat, mawkish, "the worst company in the world," as Chesterfield tells his son, that

The qualities rare in a bee that we meet,
In an epigram never should fail;
The body should always be little and sweet,
And a sting should be left in its tail.

Now it is of course unquestionable that for us, as for Martial, it was the Greeks who invented and named the epigram; it would perhaps seem courteous, therefore, if not compulsory, to allow the *Greek Anthology* some share in determining its nature. Unfortunately, however, we find in the *Anthology* no precise definition of the epigram; no use of even the word, epigram, in the proem of Meleager's *Garland,* a collection of short poems forming the basis of our *Greek Anthology;* no evidence that the Greek epigram became, until very late, a fixed literary type; no certainty that absolutely all the writers included in the *Anthology* would have been willing to call absolutely all their contributions epigrams. But despite these difficulties, let us look into the *Anthology* itself,

[14]

and, endeavouring to avoid poems which their writers might have refused to term epigrams, see whether it sanctions the diversity of form and content found in our modern epigram, and whether it justifies the extremists in either of those groups of critics.

If the best merit be to lose life well,
　To us beyond all else that fortune came:
In war, to give Greece liberty, we fell,
　Heirs of all time's imperishable fame.[1]

Here lapped in hallowed slumber Saon lies,
Asleep, not dead; a good man never dies.[2]

Cruel is death, — nay, kind! He that is ta'en
　Was old in wisdom, though his years were few;
Life's pleasure he has lost; escaped life's pain;
　Nor wedded joys nor wedded sorrows knew.[3]

As we turn the pages of the *Anthology* we soon learn that such poems are examples, centuries apart, of the earliest and most enduring type of Greek epigram, the commemorative inscription on tomb, or cenotaph, or shrine, or statue. So far, at least, we surely may trust the originators of the term, epigram, and accept the epitaph, whether composed by a Simonides, a

Martial, or a Pope, as one of its thoroughly accredited forms. We may next discover that the writers of the *Anthology* very speedily took the short step from the actual epitaph to the tiny poem mourning some dear one lately or long since gone. And a most memorable discovery it will be, if it chances to bring us for the first time to those exquisite lines of Callimachus upon his brother poet Heracleitus, now lying " a handful of grey ashes, long, long ago at rest." Little elegies such as this we find early and late in the *Anthology*. Clearly then, Landor's *Rose Aylmer,* so much admired by Lamb,

> A*h, what avails the sceptred race,*
>   A*h, what the form divine!*
> W*hat every virtue, every grace!*
>   R*ose Aylmer, all were thine.*
> R*ose Aylmer, whom these wakeful eyes*
>   M*ay weep, but never see;*
> A *night of memories and of sighs*
>   I *consecrate to thee,*

even Wordsworth's,

> S*he dwelt among the untrodden ways,*

may quite as well be called epigrams as lyrics, if Greek precedent has full weight.

From epitaphs and elegies such as these we find the Greek epigrammatists taking other short steps, to the pensive epigram on death and to the reflective epigram on the nature and conduct of life. Common creeds we find expressed, and individual ideals, snatches of philosophical theory, of ethical system, counsels of courage and counsels of despair.

Naked I reached the world at birth;
   Naked I pass beneath the earth.
Why toil I then in vain distress,
   Seeing the end is nakedness? [4]

In bed we laugh, in bed we cry,
   And born in bed, in bed we die;
The near approach a bed may show
   Of human bliss to human woe. [5]

I strove with none, for none was worth my strife.
   Nature I loved, and, next to Nature, Art;
I warmed both hands before the fire of life;
   It sinks, and I am ready to depart. [6]

It would not be easy for any of us who were unacquainted with these three poems to say which one comes straight from the *Anthology*, is a Greek epigram; it should not be hard for us, therefore, to admit that the other two are properly termed epigrams, even though the admission commits us to accepting under the same name a host of other modern poems, short, meditative, often sombre, without "sting," of course, and without even any notable "point."

The writers of the *Anthology* next turned, we may assume, to epigrams on the enjoyable aspects and elements of life, epigrams that at least in subject are often hardly more than occasional poems, fugitive pieces, on incidents or emotions, on people or animals, on the marvels of nature or the works of man. Conspicuous amongst them, and the most beguiling amongst them, we may think, are the love lyrics — for lyrics many of them may quite as well be called, except that they are usually written, as is generally true of the poems of the *Anthology,* in the elegiac metre. As a whole they appear to be exquisite trifles, rhapsodical or fantastic, gay or whimsical, like Plato's,

My star, thou gazest on the stars: O would that I might be
The starry sky, so gaze might I with myriad eyes on thee! [7]

or like Strato's,

> *If I kiss you, do you find*
> *Wrong and outrage in it?*
> *You may punish me in kind;*
> *Kiss me then this minute!* [8]

Lovers pale, and wan, and all forlorn; lovers elated, jubilant, ecstatic; lovers bubbling with pretty compliments or captivating vows; lovers of every sort we find, in short, save those who show much promise of marrying and settling down as sober, respectable family men, contented and devoted. So many of the dainty, ingenious little creations that charm us in the *Hesperides,* for instance, are just such epigrams as these, though there they masquerade under other names. Yet by no means all of these Greek love songs seem to come from the head rather than from the heart. Meleager, for example, sometimes rises from flowery fantasy to tender rapture:

> *White violets blow, the daffodils*
> *Come forth to greet the shower,*
> *And ranging far across the hills*
> *The lilies are aflower.*

[19]

And now to every lover dear,
  The fairest flower that blows,
Doth sweet Zenophila appear,
  Persuasion's perfect rose.

Ye meads, why boast your tresses fair
  And laugh at rivalry?
Sweet are the garlands that ye bear,
  But sweeter far is she.[9]

It would seem as if no one of catholic taste could be blind to the felicity and grace of such selections from the *Anthology* as we have so far considered. They are " ancient gems " indeed, and the " modern settings " given them by men like Andrew Lang, Symonds, Shelley, Leigh Hunt, Moore, Cowper, Thomas Campbell, to say nothing of men less known but no less successful in their translations, have made many of them real contributions to English poetry. Our present purpose, however, is not so much to discover the *Anthology* as to discover whether it sanctions the various types of modern epigram and whether it supports either of the two groups of critics. We seem forced to admit that it does sanction nearly every kind of epigram except the kind we originally supposed to be the only kind. And we should be glad to admit that that phil-Hellenic group of critics does not exaggerate the charm of this collection of poems, which has proved so rich a quarry for so many of our most delightful epigrammatists and lyrists, both. The other group we should rather pity than censure.

But as we read still further, we perceive that the most zealous champions of the *Anthology* go too far. " In its home the epigram is distinguished by its sweet, direct, and frank simplicity. It is lively, without guile; and pointed, without intent to vex or offend." " It is elevated in thought, and has a lapidary concision." Now we have observed that the Greek epigram does have, comparatively speaking, a "lapidary concision," though it does not always have especial "point." But "elevated in thought;" "lively, without guile;" "pointed, without intent to vex or offend"? Always? Let us see:

> *Mycilla dyes her locks, 'tis said,*
>   *But 'tis a foul aspersion;*
> *She buys them black, they therefore need*
>   *No subsequent immersion,*[10]

writes Lucilius;

Manton gave five a clyster, five a purge,
  To five a liniment, on five a call;
  There was one night, one doctor thus for all,
One hearse, one grave, one Hades, and one dirge,[11]

writes Nicharchus. In what respect are these Greek epigrams more elevated or less offensive than Martial's,

To that hair and those teeth, Laelia, give not a
    thought.
But that eye you still have, Laelia! Eyes can't be
    bought,[12]

or than those familiar lines on the physicians of George the Third,

The king employed three doctors daily —
Willis, Haberden, and Baillie —
All exceedingly skilful men,
Baillie, Willis, Haberden:
But doubtful which most sure to kill is —
Baillie, Haberden, or Willis?

We find that there are somewhat wiser defenders of the sweetness of the *Anthology*, who, though uttering no such absurd, unqualified generalizations as those just quoted, yet contend that the Greek epigrams of the " best period " are stingless and that we have no right to consider the degenerate lampoons of later times as really Greek at all. Is not this rather like saying that certain features of Victorian literature are un-English merely because they are not found in Elizabethan literature? One of the glories of the *Anthology,* moreover, and a glory which we see these same critics prompt to proclaim, is that everywhere in it, everywhere, separated by centuries of time and circumstance, are found perfect little jewels of verse. But conclusive, it seems to us, is the fact that some of the early writers, some of the writers whom these critics most esteem, have given us some very biting epigrams indeed. It was Demodocus, in the fifth century B.C., who wrote, apparently in imitation of his predecessor, Phocylides,

> *The race Cilician is bad all through,*
> *Except Cinyras; he's Cilician, too,*[13]

the original of Porson's well-known

> *The Germans in Greek*
> *Are sadly to seek;*
> *Not five in five score,*
> *But ninety-five more, —*
> *All, save only Hermann,*
> *And Hermann's a German.*

[23]

It was Callimachus, in the third century B.C., who wrote not only some of the loveliest poems in the whole *Anthology*, but also wrote,

" Timon, now you're dead and buried, tell me, since
    the truth you know,
  Which is really more unpleasant, life above or
    life below? "
" Life below is more distasteful; and — if I the
    truth must tell —
'Tis because, though you survive, Sirs, there are
    more like you in Hell." [14]

It was Meleager, the tender love poet, who wrote and included in his *Garland*, the nucleus of the whole *Anthology*, an epigram [15] quite as stinging, and disgusting, as almost any one of Martial's. So when we come to Lucilius and Nicharchus, Ammianus and Palladas, and to the other writers who contribute the hundreds of stinging epigrams in the *Anthology*, it is clear that we are reading no strange, amorphous, un-Greek writers, whatever be their date or race, but only writers who give us liberally, no doubt under Roman influence, a type of epigram uncommon, though not at all unknown, in the earlier part of the collection.

Now we may agree that the Greeks showed

their genius less in the composition of this satirical type of epigram than in the other and
prevailing types. But surely it is somewhat
ambiguous to say, without explanation, as do
certain serious-minded lovers of " Greek deli-
cacy " and haters of " Roman venom," that
the " best " things in the *Anthology* are sweet
and graceful. This is much like saying that the
" best " figures in a Doré picture of Heaven
and Hell are the angels. The devils may be
quite as good devils. The laments of such
critics, too, that Martial and the modern epigrammatists have followed what is worst in the
Anthology, rather than what is best, so prosti-
tuting a pure, sweet, lovely creation, seem but
idle tears. Quite apart from the fact that we
have seen the prostitution beginning with the
Greeks themselves, and quite apart from the
fact that many, very many, epigrams of Martial and of modern epigrammatists are excellent
examples of the " best " Greek type, this large
fact appears to have escaped them, that a host
of modern poets such as Campion, Sidney,
Wyat, Lodge, Lylye, Jonson, Waller, Crashaw,
Carew, Herrick, and Moore, to mention a few
of our own English favorites merely, have
written hundreds of poems inspired by what is

" best " in the *Anthology,* only to call them by some other name than epigrams. We may look through a collection of modern " epigrams " and conclude that the " best " of the *Anthology* has had insufficient influence. Before despairing of modern judgment, however, we should examine also a collection of modern " lyrics." Our " epigram's " loss has been our " lyric's " gain. It has been not so much a decline in taste as a difference in terminology.

Yet why should there be such reluctance to admit that otherwise reputable Greeks would write a satirical or flippant little poem, and call it an epigram? And why should anyone resent the presence of such clever, amusing skits even in an *Anthology,* most of whose epigrams are of a different sort?

Olympius, you said you'd bring
  A horse; why don't you do it?
'Tis a fair tail; but is that thing
  A horse that's hanging to it? [16]

Proclus can't wipe his nostrils when he pleases,
  His nose so long is, and his arm so short;
Nor ever cries, " God bless you! " when he sneezes;
  He cannot hear so distant a report. [17]

Light lie the earth, Nearchus, on thy clay,
That so the dogs may easier find their prey.[18]

Not such poor things, of their kind, surely, —
and essentially their own! There is at least
some virtue in variety, and Palladas' lines on
the parvenu,

Fortune advanc'd thee in thine own despight,
To prove how boundless, e'en on such, her might,[19]

Nicharchus' lines on the miser,

The stingy wretch had hang'd himself today,
But for the halter that he grudg'd to pay,[20]

should hardly offend us in the *Anthology* more
than Coleridge's couplet,

Swans sing before they die — 'twere no bad thing
Should certain persons die before they sing,

in the volume that contains *Christabel* and
Kubla Khan.

No, the Greek epigram cannot, and should
not, be limited as some of its admirers wish.
Usually graceful, delicate, ingenious, frequently ending not even with a point, but only
with a slight increase of emphasis or emotion,

it is often, also, merely miniature satire, sometimes simply amusing incident narrated in verse; usually dependent upon happiness of thought, it occasionally leans very heavily indeed upon pun or word play. In short, the *Anthology* is not exclusively " A Paradise of Dainty Devices; " it is also the very earthly palaestra of ancient wits who knew a surprisingly large proportion of the verbal holds and falls, feints and knock-outs which are in vogue today. There is only one real feature of Martial's epigrams which the *Anthology* does not justify — their occasionally excessive length. There is only one real feature of modern epigrams which the *Anthology* and Martial combined do not justify — their more than occasionally slipshod composition. The Greeks seem almost never to have forgotten the inscriptional origin of the epigram and two of its consequent qualities, polish and brevity — no such brevity as Cyrillus wished,

> *Two lines complete the epigram — or three:*
> *Write more; you aim at epic poetry* [21] —

still, brevity. Martial at least never forgot the first quality. And we, well, we, after showing them all possible courtesy and charity can at

[28]

any rate commit impossible epigrams to the asylum of Humorous Verse.

What, then, is the epigram? Most of us long to house vagrant facts within some cozy generalization. It is a very laudable desire, on the whole, though its gratification is sometimes rather hard on the facts. It would be delightful if this long discussion inevitably led to a really adequate epigrammatic definition of the epigram, complete, yet compact. But it does not. In Greek, Latin, and modern literature, in all three, though in varying proportions, the epigram may be the solemn epitaph or some savage travesty; it may be a neat compliment or a satirical thrust; it may be, in content, a dainty love poem, an elegy, an amusing incident, a moral or philosophical reflection, a fugitive piece, an occasional poem on "some single striking idea or circumstance," often hardly to be distinguished from the lyric. But no matter what be its content, we may usually expect it to be reasonably short and to end with some graceful, ingenious, pointed, weighty, witty, or satirical turn of thought to which its preceding lines lead up; we may always expect it to end with at least some rather special emphasis:

Like a woman, plump or slender,
Deep or shallow, gay or tender,
With a laugh or with a tear for human woes;
Like a woman, wise or witty,
Sweet or sour, or plain or pretty,
It is sure to have an interest in its close.

The common assumption with which we began, that it can be disposed of as merely " a short poem ending with a playful or vicious thrust at somebody or something," is a part, small but real, of our large legacy from that Roman poet whose name already has so often been invoked.

II. MARTIAL

CORDUBA, Calagurris, Gades, Bilbilis — the old classical names mean little to our really up-to-date tourist in Spain. Spain is so full of a number of things, caves, cathedrals, toreadors, Carmencitas. Even when our tourist knows some of these cities and towns by their modern names, visits them, reads red books about them, hears their citizens, perhaps, in expansive mood, rehearse their ancient glories, he is seldom tremendously thrilled by learning that they were the birthplaces of Seneca and of Lucan, of Quintilian, of Columella, of Martial. What matter if these worthies did belong to the great Spanish school of Roman Literature? Like Mark Twain's mummy, they are probably dead, and their school no doubt is closed.

Well, more momentous events than the nativity of Columella indubitably have occurred in Spain. But as for the others of that group — when Seneca and Lucan are sunk Lethewards under memorials of Moors and memories of Cordovan leather, when Calagurris and Bilbilis are merely so much ploughland and pasture, one may feel at least a mild regret that, in this swaggering age of travel, more preliminary excursions are not made to local bookshops. Yet one frequently finds that the only Martials known even to the bookshop clerk are John and Andrew. Marcus Valerius Martial, the greatest epigrammatist who ever lived — surely Lessing was right! — is apt to be as extinct, for him, as the poet's own beloved Bilbilis and Boterdum, Buradon and Vativesca, though dozens of writers, whose works he glibly proffers, owed more to that Martial than they could conveniently repay even by mere acknowledgment.

A town in northeastern Spain, in Aragon, near modern Saragossa, the Salo river plashing at the foot of its hilly streets and soon to swell the rushing Ebro, Pyrenees in the distance, in the foreground fruitful farms and forests filled with game, Bilbilis was richly decked with rural honours. A manufacturing town, too, it was, though Martial very likely erred on the side of loyalty in asserting that its armories rivalled those of Noricum and Chalybes. Nor

was it simply a thriving western community, a
Gopher Prairie of the Empire. Among its
sturdy residents of old Celtiberian and Roman
legionary stock were some, like the poet's
friend, Licinianus, who were not only good fel-
lows, hale and hearty, the Squire Westerns and
Mr. Wardles of another day, but also cultured
gentlemen. It is not strange that in his later
weariness of Rome's costly necessities, fugitive meals, jangling activities, smart insinceri-
ties, and social drudgeries, the epigrammatist's
thoughts so often reverted longingly to his native Bilbilis, with its beauty, abundance, in-
formality and content.

Martial was born about 40 A.D. Bilbilis kept
the tenour of its way. Even Martial's parents,
unlike Horace's father, seem not to have regarded their son as perhaps destined for
greater, or different, things. Conversely, if one
may judge from the rather dubious evidence
of an epigrammatist's silence in such a matter,
their son, unlike Horace, seems not to have
been especially impressed by his parents. He
mentions them by name only once,[22] if at all,
and a second allusion [23] to them is merely a
whimsical protest at the financial inadequacy of
the liberal education which they had given him

— " My father was a fool when he sent me to school," as Henry Fielding translates one line. Very likely they died when he was young and no great significance can be attached to his silence concerning them. It is clear enough that he was freeborn, and born in a fairly comfortable home. Bilbilis always connoted to him, in later years, soul-satisfying meals and soul-inviting leisure; moreover, such an excellent education as his almost certainly involved the expense of schooling in some larger town of the province.

It would be interesting to know under just what circumstances Martial, in his middle twenties, set off to that Rome, back from which Pliny the Younger was to help pay his way thirty-four years afterward. Probably, like many another country youth of boundless ambition and limited funds, in those days and in these, he knew of others who had fared well in the metropolis, felt that his own talents demanded a larger sphere, bundled together his belongings, very compactly, and arrived at the city, somehow, eventually. Bilbilis apparently gave him no special send-off, Rome no notable welcome. Perhaps his own later greeting of a certain Sextus was reminiscent:

Well! Well! Sextus! Left the farm?
  Explain your presence, do!
What reason, hope, or horoscope
  Fills Rome with wights like you?

You say you'll be a Cicero?
  Surprising legal bent?
Your Civis, too, had that in view —
  And, almost, earned his rent.

Indeed? You'll be a poet, then?
  Make Virgil's verse seem flat?
See those chaps, those, in threadbare clothes!
  They're Virgils all — verb sat.

Oho! You'll court aristocrats?
  My friend, you come too late.
Just three men say they eat that way;
  The rest are losing weight.

You mean to stay? You want advice
  On how to stay and thrive?
Well — in your ear! A good man here
  Needs luck to stay alive.[24]

Whether or not Sextus stayed long is unknown. Martial did stay, stayed from about
64 A.D. throughout the principates of Nero,
Galba, Otho, Vitellius, Vespasian, Titus, Domitian, and Nerva. Those were hard times, mostly,

for a literary provincial without money, without family connections, and without the inward characteristics and compensations of Stoic, Cynic, or saint. Nero rather enjoyed poets, but they readily became subject to his somewhat capricious and thoroughly dangerous dislikes. For some time, moreover, after the luckless conspiracy of Piso, in 65 A.D., which swept away so many of Martial's fellow countrymen, and probable patrons, such as the Senecas and Lucan, it is unlikely that a new arrival from Spain would be eager to engage public or imperial attention. Galba, Otho, and Vitellius were too busy fighting and feasting to find time for the other amenities of life, nor during that year of anarchy was there a strong temptation for anyone to lift his head too high. Martial so far had surely fallen on evil days. But Vespasian was at least a steady, untemperamental sort of person who wished well to art and literature, albeit he was disinclined to waste his substance on their devotees. It is rather remarkable that, during his decade as emperor, Martial still seems to have evaded publication.

What he was doing during those first fifteen years at Rome can only be guessed. Then, no doubt, as later, he earned a living, such as it was, as a client, a dependent upon men of wealth and prominence — their wealth and prominence being popularly judged by the number and quality of their followers. He was certainly keeping his eyes open during those years, studying his city and its life, high and low, good and bad, as no other poet and few other writers of any sort, ever did before, or since. Dickens knew low and middle-class London; Martial knew Rome entire. Nor can it be supposed that such gifts of observation and expression as he possessed lay completely dormant till he was forty years of age. Epigrams of his, similar to those in the fifteen books we have, if not some of those in the fifteen books themselves, surely must have circulated among his friends and patrons long before he published anything of which we actually know.

In the year 80 A.D., however, when Titus dedicated the Coliseum with a series of splendid and sanguinary games, Martial took occasion to gain a wider recognition by publishing his *Liber Spectaculorum*. It is not much of a book. A Roman holiday at the amphitheatre, no matter how much credit it reflected upon the management, may point a moral but seldom can adorn a tale, for us. We are not in sym-

pathy with any "grand, moral battle-ax en-
gagements," any "chaste and elegant general
slaughter," and even a Caesarean operation,
performed upon a sow in the arena, seems nowadays a highly unpromising theme for verse.
But Roman ears, like Roman eyes and stom-
achs, were robustious. The publication of this
book, and, a few years later,[25] of the *Xenia* and
Apophoreta, two books of serviceable, catch-
penny couplets to accompany Saturnalian gifts
and dinner party souvenirs, did make him favorably and widely known. Thereafter, as book
followed book [26] in almost annual succession,
he had little anxiety as to the degree and per-
manence of his fame. Few poets, in fact, have
audibly been more aware of their own enduring
distinction, or more ingenuously pleased with
it.

Here, yes, here, is the man you read and look for —
Martial, known by repute the whole world over,
Known for epigrammatic booklets, short and clever.
You have granted to him, attentive reader,
While he yet is alive and conscious of it,
Honour such as but few dead poets gather.[27]

Honour, however, or "post-obits," as Byron
translates it, brought him more compliments

than comforts. The *ius trium liberorum,* with
its special exemptions and privileges, and the
rank of *tribunus militum,* giving him the rights
of a Roman knight, honours which came to him
from Titus and Domitian, were all very well,
and let him laugh from above at childless lib-
ertines trying to avoid taxation, or at parvenus
claiming equestrian seats at the theatre; but
what he really needed was a patient, solicitous,
persevering Maecenas. He knew very well that
man does not live by bread alone, and to be
on friendly terms with almost everybody of
worth and importance, men like Quintilian,
Nerva, Stella, Avitus, Silius Italicus, Sura,
Pliny the Younger, was pleasant; but the presents from his many wealthy friends and patrons were too strictly casual to make life
continuously blissful. Their tiles for his cot-
tage and togas for his person never seemed to
arrive quite on time, or together.

Modern sympathy cannot readily be evoked
for the financial straits of an able-bodied man
who so undeniably was of a Bohemian propen-
sity; yet the vocations which a Roman gentleman could follow, without loss of social stand-
ing, were very few, and almost all of them
demanded capital or influence. Martial might

have practiced law; maybe he did for a time, without enthusiasm or success. But for gentlemen in distress the great profession at Rome was clientship. A very, very early morning call upon your patron, or patrons; a long wait, perhaps, in his atrium; then (worse luck!) membership in his cortège, if he so desired, when he fared forth; finally a fee of about a shilling, at least, for your services, with occasional meals and gifts thrown in, and hopes of a substantial legacy. It was not so bad — unless one were a little liberal as a sleeper, or a little conservative as a courtier. The profession offered perhaps more ease than dignity in Martial's decadent day, but after all, nearly everybody was, or had been, somebody's client in some degree, and Martial, with his talents and personality and fame must have secured the profession's maximum of ease, of dignity, and of emolument.

Macaulay, admitting that he memorized three hundred and sixty of Martial's best lines, granting that he " sometimes runs Catullus himself hard," proceeds to criticize him for his mendicant adulation. He strives to make allowances and to speak temperately, yet does not quite succeed in understanding the epigram-

matist's nature and position. Men of letters at
Rome very early had had their patrons. It
was the accepted thing. Virgil and Horace, for
instance, had had little hesitation in accepting
such patronage. If, through no fault of Martial's, there was no longer some *one* kind patron
to bless, adequately and cordially, each gray
goose quill, it was not too unreasonable or unbecoming for a poor literary gentleman to conduct himself like any other poor gentleman and
seek the many lesser patrons who were avail-
able. Books brought no such income as they
do in this day of copyrights and royalties, nor
should very many of our own writers, for that
matter, previous to the nineteenth century, entirely escape our condemnation, if we damn
Martial too heartily for sycophancy. At worst,
he simply took for granted the business ethics,
the crass give and get, of the whole abominable
system. For many of his patrons, men like
Priscus, Stella, Pliny, even Regulus, he undoubtedly had a very real respect or liking —
albeit friendship with both Pliny and Regulus
was a triumph of tact and catholicity of taste.
When he eulogizes such men he may very well
have been quite as sincere as the average eulo-
gist in this imperfect world. When he intimates

that a little memorial is in order, he does it so coolly or deftly, so jocularly or banteringly, so unlike Mr. Dorrit, that it seems to be but a part of the day's work for an epigrammatist.

I am broke, my dear Regulus. All I can do
Is dispose of your gifts. May I sell some to you? [28]

Bishop Hall was certainly more discerning than Macaulay —

While thread-bare Martiall turns his merry note
To beg of Rufus a cast winter-coate.

It *was* a merry note, good epigrammatic material, and if the returns either exceeded or fell short of his expectations, there was more good epigrammatic material. Patrons who were niggardly, exacting, tiresome, vicious, undesirable generally, had every opportunity to know precisely what he thought of them, even though he used fictitious names; the bibacious Pollio, for instance:

When drunk at night you promise gifts,
  But none appears next day.
Instead of evening exhibitions,
  Give a matinée, [29]

or the supercilious Pontilianus:

> I *always greet you, but you never greet me*
> *When we meet at a house or a store.*
>> *Since I get no reply,*
>> *Let me wish you good-bye,*
> *Till we meet — on that beautiful shore.*[30]

Indeed, much more visible than any "mendicant adulation" in Martial is his nonchalant ridicule of the very class of men and of the system that gave him a living.

Martial's very ample compliments for his monarchs, Domitian included, which so scandalized Addison and which good Robert Burton terms "the kind of praise that drives men mad," were again merely part of a convention accepted not only by Martial but by Quintilian, Seneca, Statius, and, allowing for chronological and racial differences in modes of expression, accepted by many honoured English poets, as well, stalwart Ben Jonson among them:

> *Martial, thou gav'st far nobler epigrams*
> *To thy Domitian, than I can my James;*
> *But in my royal subject I pass thee,*
> *Thou flatter'dst thine, mine cannot flatter'd be.*

For that matter, many of the epigrammatist's own imperial encomiums were later to be lav-

ished on English monarchs by Wither and
Davies, Prior, Dryden, and Crashaw. Martial
played no heroic rôle under Domitian, nor did
Juvenal; he may be charged with gross flattery
of Domitian living, but he should not be
charged, as he sometimes is, with violent abuse
of Domitian dead. His hardest, and almost his
only, words about the deceased emperor are
that he was a *durus princeps* and that those
were *mala tempora*.

No, the only serious charge that can be
brought against the epigrammatist is the ob-
scenity of his epigrams; and even here it makes
a large difference who the plaintiff is.[31] Robert
Louis Stevenson was one of many men who
have discovered for themselves that Martial is
usually quite decent, after all. As a matter of
fact, only about one fifth of his fifteen hundred
epigrams are open to objection — but a large
proportion of that fifth are very open indeed.
At his worst he undeniably is an expert in
pornography, innocuously funny though he
often makes it, and there is very real need of
the Graglia version to which less hardy translators may occasionally fly for refuge, so long
as Italy does not regard the practice as a *casus
belli*. To be sure he does allege, like Catullus

and Ovid, that his life is chaste though his page be wanton, which is somewhat in his favour, even as an unsupported statement; but Tennyson was quite right in protesting that a poet's " verses fly much further than he does." It is a fact, too, that the epigram was traditionally licentious. " For my free plainness of speech, that is, for the language of the epigram, I should apologize if the example were mine. But so Catullus writes, so Marsus, so Pedo, so Gaetulicus — so everyone who is read through." [32] Those who can forgive the indecencies of churchmen, such as Hall and Donne and Herrick and Swift, may perhaps pardon the first-century wit for too often being like the " wits of Charles " in Johnson's Prologue: " They pleased their Age, and did not strive to mend."

But enough of the negative. Martial had a sufficient share of positive virtues. It took a good deal of courage to stay in Rome at all after the Pisonian conspiracy had carried off his friends and patrons. It took a good deal of self-confidence to remain there during the many lean and lowly years preceding the publication of his first book. It took a good deal of optimism to be able for many years more to

see the amusing side of life, to speak of his
own poverty facetiously or wryly, rather than
bitterly, while living from hand to mouth and
occupying a garret three flights up. It took a
good deal of serenity to be able to smile at himself after all his ability and fame had finally
secured him merely a waterless town house, a
miniature country place, and a span of mules,
with upkeep and clothing still to seek. It took
a good deal of real fellowship to be on friendly
terms with nearly everybody of parts and consequence in Rome, a good deal of real sincerity
to win from a man like the younger Pliny a
reputation for *candor,* a good deal of basic
moral soundness to enjoy, and be enjoyed by,
a Juvenal and a Quintilian. Many of his little
tributes to friends are quite as clear evidence
of his own quality as of theirs:

> *Your birthday, April first, is here,*
> *A day I love, yes, Quintus dear,*
> *Love much as my own natal day —*
> *The first of March — and well I may.*
> *Red letter days are both for me,*
> *Both days I welcome gratefully.*
> *One gave me life, dear Quintus, — true;*
> *But one gave more, it gave me you.*[33]

Or again:

> If *there be friend such as those former few*
> *Whom old-time faith and ancient story knew;*
> If *there be sage, each science his, each art,*
> *Yet simple still in goodness, and in heart;*
> If *there be champion of truth and right,*
> *Who prays in secret as he prays in sight;*
> If *there be man whose own soul is his stay,*
> *Then, Decianus, you are he, I say.*[34]

No hero himself, he could appreciate and applaud genuine nobility of spirit and action in others, without belittling analysis or hesitated dislike or civil leer. He had no exalted, and remote, ideals of altruism and self-sacrifice, but judged by ordinary human practice, he was sane, well-balanced, tolerant, and uncommonly free from the petty meannesses which ravage the higher ideals of most of us. He struggled with no great spiritual problems, was harassed by no visions, was carried away by no fine moral enthusiasms, had no great moral earnestness, even, but he did have an extraordinarily keen perception of what are considered to be material realities:

Julius, the things that make for ease
And happiness in life are these:

Lands left me, not acquired with toil;
Unfailing fuel; kindly soil;
No suits; light work; mind void of whims;
Good constitution; healthy limbs;
Frank thoughts; plain board; congenial friends;
Meals that, with Plenty, Mirth attends;
Nights with good cheer, not drinking, sped;
A glad, but not immodest bed;
Sound sleep that makes the darkness fly;
Content with life, if I be I,
Without the fear, or wish, to die.[35]

This epigram, combined with the noble lines on Antonius Primus,

Blest in his retrospect of harmless years,
He dreads not death as Lethe's stream he nears.
No day that he recalls inspires regret;
Not one his conscience wishes to forget.
Memory to virtuous men fresh years can give:
T' enjoy the past in life is twice to live,[36]

carries us as far as he goes in philosophical or moral meditation — not very far, to be sure, yet certainly far enough to refute the statement that " a certain intolerance of hypocrisy is the nearest approach Martial ever makes to moral feeling." [37]

After thirty-four years at Rome, years during which the duties of a client grew constantly more irksome and the memories of Bilbilis more grateful, Martial, still poor, still unmarried, but now famous, returned to Bilbilis where a certain Marcella, a Spanish lady, of whom he speaks with affection and esteem, gave him a pleasant estate on which he was able to live in the comfortable, informal, leisurely fashion that had seemed to him so perfect, viewed from Rome. For a time it was perfect; but he had been spoiled for small-town limitations. Apologizing for his long silence, he wrote to a friend: " I miss that audience of my fellow-citizens to which I had grown accustomed, and seem to myself a pleader in a strange court; for whatever is popular in my small books my hearers inspired. That subtlety of judgment, that inspiration of the subject, the libraries, theatres, meeting-places, where pleasure is a student without knowing it — to sum up all, those things which fastidiously I deserted, I regret, like one desolate. Added to this is the back-biting of my fellow townsmen, and envy ousting judgment, and one or other evilly disposed persons — a host in a tiny place — a circumstance against which it is difficult every day to keep a good stomach; do not wonder, therefore, that occupations have been cast aside in repugnance which I used to follow with ardour." [38]

"The world of Rome was an open book before him. He read the text, fathomed its import, and wrote his commentary upon it in brilliant and telling phrases, and in a literary form of which he was undoubtedly the master." [39] *Hominem pagina nostra sapit.* Had he spent fewer years in the city, he might have returned to Bilbilis to find not only content, but inspiration. An ancient *Cranford,* described by one who saw so clearly and could speak so whimsically as well as so pungently, would surely have been another volume which men would "read and bear to distant lands long after the rock-hewn sepulchre of Messala had crumbled, and Licinus' towering monument was dust."

But Martial wrote only one book — another book of epigrams still distinctly Roman — in his self-imposed exile, and there in Bilbilis he died, not later than 104 A.D. Of all the friends and readers who had done him homage while he lived, only one has left us any record of his death, and that one, the same admirable Pliny who had provided his viaticum to Spain, concerned as he always was with his own posthumous fame, voiced a regretful fear that Martial's verse, in which he himself was praised, might not endure.

III. CENTURIES OF EPIGRAMS

I T IS seldom absolutely safe in any age to predict that this or the other contemporary writer will survive. Martial was pointed out to foreign visitors, plagiarized at Rome and abroad, read and sung all over the Roman Empire, yet Pliny may be pardoned for suspecting that the poet's assurance of helping to convey his benefactor's name to posterity might miscarry. But eighteen hundred years have passed, and we have ample evidence that Martial, unlike some ancient authors of even greater worth, his own beloved Catullus, for example, was entirely unknown to readers, and to writers, in not a single century following his death.

In the second century he was the " Virgil " of Verus Caesar, the adopted son and intended successor of Hadrian. It was hardly an instance, however, of *laudari a viro laudato*. Spartianus, in the third century, speaks of Verus' love for the epigrammatist, and, in the fourth, Lampridius quotes one of his poems in his biography of Alexander Severus. In the fourth century, too, St. Jerome and Martianus Capella, the encyclopedist of North Africa, use him once or twice, while Ausonius, the learned rhetor and poet, tutor and friend of the emperor Gratian, borrowed from him freely. A man who loved the old pagan culture and strove to reinstate it, Gennadius Torquatus, made a recension of the epigrammatist in the fifth century, and many grammarians of both this and the century before went to the epigrams for purposes of illustration. Sedulius, author of a Bible epic, the *Paschale Carmen,* Luxorius, living in Africa under the Vandal kings, and Alcimus Avitus, the scholarly bishop of Vienne, knew and occasionally imitated or quoted Martial; Arator and Gildas apparently were acquainted with the epigrams, though a warmer admirer of them was the court poet, Venantius Fortunatus. But it was Sidonius Apollinaris, the Gallic nobleman, bishop, poet and letter writer, who was the epigrammatist's most eminent imitator among the writers of the fifth and sixth centuries. In the seventh century we come to that prodigy of industry and learning, Isidore, bishop of Seville, whose *Etymologies,* or *Origins,* disclose very nearly the whole range of mediaeval culture. Isidore uses Martial in divers ways more than a score of times, and in the next century Theodulf, the able and cultivated bishop of Orléans, scholar and poet, incorporates a bit of Martial in his eulogy of Charlemagne, while the Venerable Bede also cites him once.

From the ninth to the fourteenth century we have manuscripts of the poet, as well as imitations of him and references to him on the part of such men as that eminent humanist, Lupus of Ferrières, Hraban, the learned abbot of Fulda, Paulus Albarus of Cordova, the Jewish defender of Christianity against Islam, Christian, the monk of Stablo, Micon of St. Riquier, one of the outstanding literary figures in the monastic life of his time — all of the ninth century — Liutprand, bishop of Cremona, and Thietmar of Merseburg, author of the *Chronicles,* both tenth-century scholars, John of Salisbury and Vincentius Bellovacensis of the twelfth and thirteenth centuries, respectively. Martial had held his own very well indeed up to the fourteenth century when Boccaccio is rather gratuitously declared to have been his " discoverer." All through the centuries till Boccaccio's day " Martial " and the

" epigram " were nearly synonymous. His poems appeared in mediaeval anthologies, and a large number that were not his were ascribed to him; it is evident that many a writer was quite willing to identify himself with Martial and that many a reader was inclined to believe that a good epigram must be Martial's. Only in the limited sense of being the first " modern man " to discover the ancient epigrammatist did Boccaccio do so.

In the fifteenth century began a long line of scholar-poets who for two hundred years were to continue to produce Latin epigrams very largely inspired by Martial and very often closely imitative of him. They deserve more attention than we can give them. Their epigrams are as numerous as Catullian kisses. The great collections of Gruter, and even the selections published by Abraham Wright under the mellifluous title *Delitiae Delitiarum*, fairly appal one, not merely by mass but by distribution. Lawyers, doctors, professors, noblemen, priests, bishops, cardinals; scholars of Italy, the Netherlands, France, Germany, England; clients of Lorenzo the Magnificent and reformers of the school of Luther and Melanchthon; Anselmus, Pannonius, Cordus, Muretus, Cunradinus,

Bauhusius, Paschasius, Sannazaro, Politian, Bembo, Joachim du Bellay, Beza, Stroza, Everard! Quite apart from specific imitations, of which there are many, it is quite obvious that much of the work of such men would have been left undone, had Martial never lived. Nor is their work insignificant. It not only has intrinsic value, but many of our own English poets also, such as Spenser, Milton, Jonson, Herrick, Pope, Prior, Swift, Moore, knew and profited by these Latin epigrams, whether written in what is the prevailing tone of the *Greek Anthology* or of Martial.

English writers of Latin epigrams, too, like More, Owen, Paterson, Campion, Buchanan, Herbert and Bourne, were in varying degree under the influence of Martial and often followed him closely. The vogue of Owen, in particular, was amazing. An Oxford man who became Master of the Grammar School at Warwick in the last quarter of the sixteenth century, he produced a dozen books of epigrams which met with most extraordinary favour. Acclaimed by many readers in his own day as a poet greater than Shakespeare, given burial in St. Paul's, translated into English by Thomas Harvey, hailed as the " English Martial," and for nearly a century really rivalling Martial as a model for epigrammatists throughout Europe, he is now hardly known even to students of literature. His epigrams are short, caustic, witty, and, though he frequently borrowed from the Roman poet, his debt to Martial was in the main, like Logau's, a vast general indebtedness. He brought the first-century wit quite up to date in relation to the social, political, and religious life of his own day.

To return to the fifteenth century — editions of Martial left the presses almost as soon as they began to operate. The *editio princeps* seems to be of 1471; there are several such early undated editions. The epigrams were certainly printed at Ferrara in 1471, and in 1473 at Rome by two scholars who in Latin verses at the end of the volume blushingly own to the uninspired names of Sweynheym and Pannartz. From that time forth editions and commentaries have been very numerous, and among the scholars to whom Martial owes most are Calderino, Junius, Gruter, Scriverius, Schneidewin, Friedlaender, and Lindsay.

With the printing of Martial there naturally began a new and wider interest in the epigram which was to continue through the eighteenth century. The writers of Latin epigrams, already prolific enough, perhaps, were the first to be enheartened, but epigrammatists such as Cardinal Bembo, Du Bellay and Sir Thomas More were soon to carry on Martial and the Martial tradition as well as the *Greek Anthology* and its tradition, not only in Latin but also in their own tongues, and it is the Roman poet's influence, century by century, upon some of the national literatures of the modern world that we now shall very inadequately summarize.

The fifteenth and sixteenth centuries may be taken together. In Italy, Bernardo Accolti, the great *improvvisatore* whose recitations made all Rome shut up shop and flock to hear him, frequently imitated Martial; Luigi Alamanni, whose satiric verse was so much admired by Wyat, is reminiscent of the Latin poet as well as of the *Greek Anthology;* Bernardino Baldi, mathematician, scientist, poet, the author of more than a thousand epigrams, owed Martial much, in general and in particular. In France, where classical models were to dominate so long, Mellin de Saint-Gelais and Clément Marot were frank imitators of the Roman wit. Rabelais quotes him and Montaigne quotes him, translates him, and discusses topics sug-

gested by him. Marot was translated by Paul
Schede at Heidelberg, the first important cen-
tre of humanism in Germany, but although
Martial was often edited in sixteenth-century
Germany and although many Latin epigrams
were written there in imitation of him, the
German epigram proper, apart from the *Pria-
meln,* did not begin till the century following.

In England, however, the Elizabethan period
was full of English epigrams, and full of Martial. Whether or not Warton is right in stating
that the first pointed epigram in our language
is More's "On a Student's Marriage," it is
incontestable that whoever introduced this type
of epigram into English literature had a zealous following. Martial was largely responsible.
He was anonymously translated into English
verse during Elizabeth's reign, and " The Most
Elegant and Wittie Epigrams " of Sir John
Harington, the queen's own graceless godson,
are often but unacknowledged versions of the
Latin poet. Mediocre epigrammatists would
turn off their poems by the hundred; the composition of " centuries " of epigrams was nothing to men who made untrammelled use of
Latin and Greek predecessors. Most of them,
their works never having been reprinted, are

hardly names, though a few, such as Heywood the dramatist, and Thomas Bastard with his *Chrestoleros* have been more fortunate.

But there were several late-sixteenth and early-seventeenth-century poets of greater consequence whose debt to Martial in at least certain parts of their work is very large. Sir John Davies, lawless student of law and later Lord Chief Justice elect, whose *Nosce Teipsum* causes him to be called our first didactic poet, was also called an "English Martial." His chief claim to the title is the fact that his epigrams, written in his youth, probably never would have been written at all but for Martial: in *The Lots* he imitates even the Latin poet's *Xenia* and *Apophoreta*. Quite apart from their coarseness, it would have been no great loss to literature if these poems, printed as an addition to Marlowe's translation of Ovid's *Epistles* in 1596, had perished utterly in the fire to which they, accompanying the satires of Hall and Marston, were condemned by ecclesiastical authorities in 1599 with the injunction that "no satires or epigrams be printed hereafter." John Donne was another real poet of the period who in his youth "the burning rush of swift iambics tried." Even as Dean of St. Paul's,

Donne could hardly be called mealy-mouthed. It may be that the Latin poems so long ascribed to him, and later stricken from his account, are really his. But his English epigrams, some of them very good, are much coloured by his familiarity with Martial, and not with the worst of Martial. Joseph Hall, Bishop of Exeter, who, in his twenty-third year, wrote the *Virgidemiarum*, known as the first English satires, was still another notable admirer and imitator of the Roman poet, and Henry Howard, Earl of Surrey, though primarily interested, like Wyat, in the burning sighs, frozen hearts, and scornful ways of the stock heroines of the century's amorists, enjoyed his Martial, too, as his own poems now and then attest. Whether or not Shakespeare was acquainted with the epigrammatist is doubtful: two or three instances of similarity in the expression of rather common thoughts furnish small evidence. Francis Bacon, of course, did know him, and by quotation and enlargement makes the epigram serve the essay.

It was in the seventeenth century, however, that the epigram really came into its modern own, and Martial was still the great exemplar. Even where an attempt was made to break away from the classical tradition, as in the case of Frigimelica-Roberti, the Paduan professor of medicine, the effects of that tradition still lingered. The German epigram once emerging became a torrent, and Martial, sharing his supremacy for a time with Owen, ruled its waves. Levy cites some forty German poets of the century who imitated those lays of ancient Rome which came tumbling from the presses in dozens of editions. It was Opitz who founded this German school of epigrammatists, and his *Florilegium* included about fifty translations from the books of " the Bilbilitanian." Best known of these forty poets are Weckherlin, Wernicke and Logau, the last of whom Lessing exuberantly called " the German Martial and Catullus," and " Germany's greatest poet." Logau's thousands of epigrams are not direct imitations of the Latin poet: only a score or so of real plagiarisms are to be found. But except for two great themes which Martial seldom touches, war and religion, his themes, as well as his tones and methods, are very much those of his ancient prototype, and it seems quite likely that had there been no Martial there would have been no Logau.

The conception of the epigram as being " satire in brief" lasted throughout the century in Germany. The constant appellation of this or the other caustic writer was "Deutscher Martial," or "Zweiter Martial," or "Alter Bilbilitanus." But despite the prevalence of this limited conception of the epigram and of Martial, the Latin poet was often used in other ways than to suggest a mode of ridicule. The worthy Pastor Johannes Burmeister, for instance, in his *Martial Renatus,* by printing on one page Martial's Latin and on the next a fully emancipated adaptation of his own, contrived to make the pagan poet serve a Christian purpose — *teneram iuventam ex cloaca ethnicae foeditatis ad officinam Christianae pietatis educere.*

In Spain during this century, it was the *Greek Anthology* which perhaps most influenced the epigram, yet even in Spain men like Villegas, Lope de Vega, Quevedo, and especially Francisco de la Torre, remembered their Martial, too — and their Owen. In France it was unmistakably the Latin poet, in his satiric vein, that predominated, as might be expected in a country whose court was "despotism tempered by epigram" and whose courtiers could find readers of the rhymes about painted ladies which they reeled off by the hundred on

wagers. Yet it is not merely a collection of
generously forgotten French poetasters who
turned to Martial for inspiration. Voiture,
Chapelle, Maynard, Benserade, Bussy-Rabutin
are names no longer shouted from the house-
tops, but Racine and La Fontaine and Boileau
also knew and used their copies of the Roman
wit and of Marolles' translation.

In England Martial's influence was much
the same. It was a time when " without his
point a lover durst not rage." Imitators and
translators like May, Fletcher, John Heath,
Henry Parrot, Samuel Sheppard, Thomas Ban-
croft, William Walsh, Thomas Freeman,
Bishop Corbet, and Henry King, do not now
impress us, no matter how many " centuries "
of epigrams they wrote, or what their depend-
ence upon the Roman poet. Even Fanshawe
and Quarles and John Beaumont and Sedley
and Butler, as but occasional users of the epigrammatist, seem unimpressive. But when we
find Martial appearing in Lovelace, Crashaw,
and Waller, when we see him frequently
quoted, translated and discussed by Cowley,
when we observe how often he illustrates some
point for Dryden despite Dryden's strong aver-
sion to the epigram, and when we discover that

he is the real author of many scores of lines in the poems of Ben Jonson and in the *Hesperides* of Robert Herrick, " the supreme achievement of Renaissance song," we are impressed. Even outside the realm of the epigram, so important a literary type in seventeenth-century England, Martial had a place. On some honorary medals, for instance, given to naval officers in the reign of the second Charles is the motto, *Pro Talibus Ausis;* in Fuller's *Worthies* he appears from time to time, and, introducing Shakespeare, Fuller tells us that in him " three eminent poets may seem in some sort to be compounded " — Martial, Ovid, and Plautus, the first as having a warlike name! But apart from the poets, it is Jeremy Taylor who uses Martial most often and most surprisingly. Dozens of times it is the " callous, conscienceless Roman jester " who introduces or points for Taylor some thoughtful disquisition on holy living or dying.

The eighteenth century found the epigram still flourishing and those of Martial still its criterion. In Italy, Paolo Rolli, that facile, versatile, and popular man of the world, Saverio Bettinelli, amiable gentleman and travelled teacher, Carlo Roncalli, fluent and sprightly, were copious writers of epigrams, some original and some taken from the *Anthology*, from Martial, and from the French. It was toward the end of this century that Graglia published his unblinking, unblushing translation of the poet. In Germany several translations also were made in prose and verse, and poets great and small took their turn at writing the same sort of thing. Götz and Ewald and Kretschmann, Kästner, Kleist, Gleim, and Klopstock all knew Martial, as did Goethe and Herder and Schiller, but most of them were not so indebted to him as to the *Anthology*. Lessing, however, easily the foremost German epigrammatist in the satiric style, was profoundly influenced by Martial both in theory and in practice. Of his two hundred epigrams at least a score are taken straight from the Latin poet — nearly all of them from the first three books, curiously; another score barely escape being translations, and most of the others are close to Martial in tone, method, and subject. Only two or three times does he specifically acknowledge indebtedness to his predecessor, but Martial looms so large in Lessing's whole critique of the epigram that his failure to acknowledge each imitation contributes little support to Paul Albrecht's thesis that Lessing was the greatest plagiarist in all literature. France meanwhile was producing her grist of epigrams, mostly in the Roman poet's satiric style. Lebrun, Marmontel, Rulhière, Marie-Joseph Chénier, La Harpe, Fontenelle, Panard, Boufflers — hardly more than names, again. But Piron, Voltaire, and Jean Baptiste Rousseau still live, and in them lives much of Martial.

In England, too, the composition of pointed, witty epigrams was a popular pastime. Everybody wrote them, courtiers, poets, gay young bloods, devilish young shopkeepers. Failing pen and paper, there were diamonds and window pane. " Centuries " were still poured forth; an amazing number of " Collections " were printed; and still the responsibility was largely Martial's. Several verse translations of his poems, too, were made, the best by William Hay, M. P. for Seaford, the worst by James Elphinston, a schoolmaster who could be neither persuaded nor bribed to forego his dread resolve to put in the book stalls that gory massacre of the poet, derided by Beattie, " a whole quarto of nonsense and gibberish is too much," and declared by Doctor Johnson to show " too much folly for madness, and too much madness for folly." Again, as in the previous century, we have first a group of men who loved Martial and carried him over into their own work now pretty much forgotten — Aaron Hill, " the Muses' sacred Hill," as Richardson called him, Samuel Bishop, the Head Master of Merchant Taylors' school and himself another " Martial of England," Dr. Jortin, Archdeacon of London, John Byrom, Abel Evans, Richard Graves, Fellow of All Souls' and author of *The Festoon,* Josiah Relph, Lord Hervey, Dr. Cotton, George Hardinge, Dr. Delany. Then there comes a list which looks like a roster of the century's English men of letters — Congreve, Pope, Lyttelton, Walpole, Swift, Steele, Johnson, Chesterfield, Prior, Young, Thomson, Warton, Addison, Fielding — all of whom admire, quote, translate or otherwise use the Roman poet in varying degree. Addison, for example, though temperamentally quite alien to Martial and convinced that Claudian was his peer as an epigrammatist, nevertheless quotes and translates him nearly forty times — oftener than he quotes any other Latin writers save Virgil, Horace, Ovid, and Juvenal.

Of all these epigrammatists there are three who are really great, though no one of them wrote many epigrams — Prior, Pope, and Burns. Prior confesses to having his Horace on his shelf beside him as he writes: his Martial must have been close at hand, for directly and indirectly he is much beholden to Martial both in his serious and in his frivolous moods, in his eulogies of friends and in his mockery of ladies who at critical moments are so unfortunate as to lose their eyebrows, complexion, or virtue. It is a real tribute to Martial, for unlike Herrick, whose efforts to amuse are seldom more successful than those of the elephant in Eden who " to make them sport wreath'd his proboscis lithe," Prior, both as London profligate and French ambassador, had a very lively wit of his own. The second of the three, Pope, verily lisped not only in numbers but in epigrams. Had he chosen to be solely an epigrammatist, instead of always epigrammatical, he, and not the Roman poet, would certainly be called the greatest epigrammatist of all time. He and Jonson perhaps had more real affinity with Martial than any other great English writers since Martial's day, but while Jonson quotes and adapts the Latin poet constantly, only a dozen or fifteen instances of direct indebtedness to Martial can be found in all that Pope ever wrote. Yet his crispness, keenness, precision, and polish make him a much closer stylistic successor of Martial than Jonson was. Burns depends not at all upon the Roman poet. He mentions him once in connection with Elphinston and his notorious translation:

O *thou whom Poetry abhors,*
W*hom Prose has turnèd out of doors,*
Heard'*st thou yon groan? — proceed no further,*
'*Twas laurel'd Martial calling Murther.*

But Burns' native wit and ready pen make him one of the world's great epigrammatists, both in the polished style of Martial and Pope, and in the more rough and ready style of Garrick and Goldsmith.

The polished and witty epigram of the eighteenth century in England trailed off into the humorous verse of Peter Pindar and never has been completely re-established as a proper form of verse for a great poet to cultivate. The nineteenth century had its Landor, to be sure, but few of its more eminent writers ventured far into the field of satirical epigram except Coleridge, Byron, and Moore, all of whom sometimes imitated Martial. The tradition of Peter Pindar was carried on, and instead of polished wit we have a large amount of free and easy witticism from men like Hood and Hook, Lowell and Holmes, James Smith and his brother Horace. Most of them knew Martial: the Smiths, misguidedly, even wrote a so-called *Martial in London*. An occasional translation or adaptation of some serious epigram may still be discovered in the pages of a Rogers, Hunt, or Swinburne, and we hear Emerson saying: " Nothing can be preserved which is not good; and I know beforehand that Pindar, Martial, Terence, Galen, Kepler, Galileo, Bacon, Erasmus, More, will be superior to the average intellect." The sentiment is reasonably sound, though the congeries of names is curious. It somehow reminds one of Martial's place among the names inscribed on the Boston Public Library. He is there in the company of Gaius, Ulpian, Justinian, and Suetonius, flanked on one side by Choate, Shaw, Story, Hale, and Kent, on the other by Coke, Blackstone, Brougham, Chatham, and Fox! His efforts to escape the legal profession appear to have been unavailing! To Emerson, however, Martial really was more than a name to conjure with, as is clearly proven by other passages in his essays.

[71]

In Germany, as in England, the satirical epigrams of the nineteenth century come from fewer and less distinguished men, though in both countries verse translations of Martial by minor poets appeared, from time to time. Haug, Voss, and Schlegel were still very well aware of him, and poets such as Rückert, Geibel, Uhland, Heyse, Platen, and Grillparzer occasionally wrote verses which are suggestive of him. In France the situation was much the same: the crowded day of the polished satirical epigram had passed. In Italy, however, the epigram, generally satirical, flourished through most of the century. Angelo D'Elci, that modern Cellini; De'Rossi, skilled in law and letters; Ugo Foscolo, Domenico Cervelli, abbot and teacher; Leopardi — all show some relationship to Martial. Mario Mariani, Pananti, indefatigable and witty, Giucci and Nícoli-Cristiani, a pair of industrious but moderately gifted wits, Zefirino Re, Calvelli, Montanari, Capparozzo, Baratta, diplomat and litterateur, Capozzi, Norberto Rosa, Veludo, Montaspro, Pasqualigo — the list is long of men who still composed their " centuries " of epigrams, many of them good, and many of them straight from Martial.

Writers of the twentieth century use and refer to the Latin poet even less than those of the nineteenth. Now and then appears some metrical version of selected epigrams; here or there in our verse or prose we come upon an allusion to some character he portrays, some incident he narrates, some Roman scene he pictures; and constantly in the twentieth century, as in the centuries preceding, do we find his name in the text or footnotes of those unthumbed books that have to do with life at Rome two thousand years ago. His mantle as a humorist seems to have fallen nowadays upon the " comic verse " writers and newspaper columnists whose careless, motley stanzas amuse so many myriads; his ancient reprobates now dwell in our *Spoon Rivers;* his joy in filed and trenchant diction is carried on by those coteries of prose writers with whom point's the thing. The day of his direct influence upon much of the world's writing perhaps is done, but, be that as it may, the stamp already borne by so many of the things we prize in modern literature, MADE IN ROME, might often, very often, show the added words, BY MARTIAL.

IV. PERENNIALS

FRIENDS of Martial are apt to dislike the casualness, as well as the bitterness, with which ardent lovers of the *Greek Anthology* are apt to dispose of him. " The contemporary Greek epigrammatists whose work is preserved in the *Palatine Anthology,* from Nicharchus and Lucilius to Strato, all show the same heaviness of handling and the same tiresome insistence on making a point, which prevent Martial's epigrams from being placed in the first rank. But while in any collection of Greek epigrammatic poetry these authors naturally sink to their own place, Martial, as well by the mere mass of his work — some twelve hundred pieces in all, exclusive of the cracker mottoes — as by his animation and pungent wit, set a narrow and rather disastrous type for later literature. He appealed strongly to all that was worst in Roman taste — its heavy-handedness, its admiration of verbal cleverness, its tendency toward brutality." [40]

Any literary verdict of Mackail's commands
attention. But as he was clearly too severe regarding the epigrammatist's morals, so is he
too severe respecting the quality and influence
of his epigrams. It was something of an
achievement merely to have composed " some
twelve hundred pieces," a greater achievement
to have limited himself to the field in which he
excelled, a still greater achievement to have
written more epigrams which have been re-read
and imitated than any other man who ever
lived. Furthermore, if all Martial's heavy-handedness and brutality, if all his pungent wit, if
all that is amusing, or meant to be amusing, in
Martial be stricken out, there still remains a
very large proportion of those twelve hundred
pieces; and of that remainder many, very
many, set anything but " a narrow and rather
disastrous type for later " epigrams, and lyrics.
" Tiresome insistence on making a point " is a
charge less easy to combat. Yet in a world's
literature there is perhaps room for the pointed
style, in its perfection, as for every other style;
to adapt one of the poet's own rebuttals:

> If *you are tried unduly*
> By *my tiresomeness of style,*
> Try *another's for a while.*

[75]

Some of Martial's epigrams, however, are absolutely without " point," and in many of them the point is so delicate and graceful that it should hardly hurt the most sensitive. Neither brutality, nor heavy-handedness, nor offensive point, surely, were the invariable attributes of a man who could write upon the death of a little slave girl:

Dear father and dear mother: Let me crave
Your loving kindness there beyond the grave
For my Erotion, the pretty maid
Who bears these lines. Don't let her be afraid!
She's such a little lassie — only six —
To toddle down that pathway to the Styx
All by herself! Black shadows haunt those steeps
And Cerberus the Dread who never sleeps.
May she be comforted, and may she play
About you merry as the livelong day,
And in her childish prattle often tell
Of that old master whom she loved so well.
Oh earth, bear lightly on her! 'Tis her due;
The little girl so lightly bore on you.[41]

It was reserved for modern writers, such as Weckherlin and Abel Evans, to show us that even such tender words could be burlesqued, brutalized, and made to serve the base uses of pungent wit.

There are nearly two score of these little elegies among Martial's epigrams, and not always, by any means, is the point, or the conceit, obtrusive; even when bold, it often is effective. Scorpus, the gallant young charioteer, cut off by Lachesis in his twenties:

Dum numerat palmas, credidit esse senem.[42]

John Beaumont, in saying of his brother Francis that Death

Miscounted years, and measur'd age by fame,

is only one of many modern writers — Owen, Relph, Bacon, Suckling, Thomas Harvey, Young, Drummond, Crashaw, Ben Jonson — who have made of this conceit a virtue. Hardly pointed at all, but merely weighty, are the last lines of the epigram on the slave boy Glaucia:

Immodicis brevis est aetas et rara senectus.
Quidquid amas, cupias non placuisse nimis.[43]

One of them lives in Jonson's tender epitaph upon his son:

Rest in soft peace, and ask'd say here doth lie
BEN JONSON his best piece of poetry:
For whose sake henceforth all his vows be such,
As what he loves may never like too much.

They furnished Cowley with the motto of his elegy for his friend Harvey, supplied Evelyn with material for a letter of condolence and for his *Diary*, provided Steele with a text and homily for the *Spectator*, started Pelisson and De Bussy upon a controversy; perhaps, directly or indirectly, one of them may even have suggested Shakespeare's line:

So wise so young, they say, do ne'er live long.

Jonson's tribute to Shakespeare, at any rate,

Th' applause, delight, the wonder of our stage,

seems certainly to have been suggested by Martial's tribute to the actor Latinus:

Dulce decus scaenae, ludorum fama, Latinus
Ille ego sum, plausus deliciaeque tuae.[44]

Quite in the Greek manner is the lament for Alcimus whose resting place is to be marked by no Parian stone,

But box and shady palms shall flourish here
And softest herbage green with many a tear.
Dear boy! These records of my grief receive,
These simple honours that will bloom and live;
And be, when Fate has spun my latest line,
My ashes honour'd, as I honour thine.[45]

Opitz imitates this charming elegy; Herrick remembered it when he wrote *To Laurels,* and one is reminded of it by Pope's *Elegy to the Memory of An Unfortunate Lady* whose resting place also is marked by no polished marble,

Yet shall thy grave with rising flow'rs be drest,
And the green turf lie lightly on thy breast:
There shall the morn her earliest tears bestow,
There the first roses of the year shall blow.

Sir John Roe, who has escaped foreign perils only to learn that death comes without regard for time or place, is Martial's Curiatius;[46] Herrick's " sober matron, contented with the bed of one," is Martial's matron[47] too; the Latin epitaph on Voiture and the English epitaph on Charles Churchill are modelled on that epigram of Martial's wherein are enumerated all the qualities that delight and ravish, and all of them, all

Hoc sunt condita, quo Paris, sepulchro[48] —

a form and fancy employed by Marullus and La Fontaine, by Herrick, Pope, and Swift, as well. Below Waller's portrait in the 1686 copy of his poems one reads, as about Martial's Camonius,[49] that poetry is a " maior imago; "

Lovelace translates the epigram on Porcia,[50] the wife of Brutus, and Leigh Hunt the elegy [51] on the grave where " lies little sweet Erotion; " Montaigne quotes from the epigram on the death of *mollis Otho*,[52] Dryden's " soft Otho " of *Astraea Redux*. It is probably absurd to think that Tennyson had Martial's Camonius Rufus [53] in mind when he wrote of General Gordon, " somewhere dead far in the waste Soudan," but there is no doubting the influence of Martial's four lines [54] upon the far separated graves of Pompey and his sons. What wonder such a brood was scattered even in death?

Jacere
Uno non poterat tanta ruina loco —

" So vast a ruin could not spread less wide," as Aaron Hill translates it. From the time of Beza, who applies it to Holbein's half-length portrait of Erasmus, and of Bernardo Accolti, the conceit has continued in modern use. Nor has there been less use of the epigrammatist's comment on Antony's assassination of Cicero:

What boots it thee, to silence, at such price,
One divine tongue? Think'st so to hide thy vice?
For virtue now, and murder'd Tully's sake,
All tongues inveigh and all Philippics make.[55]

[80]

Dryden, for example, applies it to Lucian and his critics, Voltaire to French critics of Cicero.

But, rather strangely, it has been still another little elegy that has been most admired and imitated by modern authors, from Weckherlin, Gryphius, and Logau to Swinburne. As Sedley renders it — badly enough, but not so badly as Relph and Lovelace and a host of others —

When Arria to her Paetus gave the steel
  Which from her bleeding side did newly part,
" For my own wound," she said, " no pain I feel;
  And yet thy wound will stab me to the heart." [56]

Montaigne tells of Arria in his *Three Good Women* and remarks, sagaciously, that " her action was much more noble in itself than the poet could express it." In the *Tatler*, Addison, too, recounts the story of Arria and pronounces the epigram " one of the best transmitted to us from antiquity." It is hardly that. Dr. Jortin was right in feeling that the immortal *Paete, non dolet* was spoiled by paraphrase. Here, at least, we should agree with Mackail that there *is* " tiresome insistence on making a point," and Gray, writing upon Mrs. Clerke,

In agony, in death, resigned
She felt the wound she left behind,

may, in this case, have been one of the contributors to that modern literature for which Martial " set a rather disastrous type."

Martial is not ordinarily a moralist. Lessing justly says of him: " Er moralisiert mehr durch Beispiele, als durch Worte." Yet as he has his parallels, and, in a number of instances, worthy parallels, to the elegies of the *Greek Anthology,* so, too, he does sometimes parallel the reflective and didactic parts of that collection. When he chose, he could compress some ethical principle, some bit of worldly wisdom, into one or two pregnant, quotable lines with all the felicity of a Seneca or Pope. It may be added that both he and Pope profited by Seneca's priority.

Refert sis bonus an velis videri.[57]

Ardua res haec est, opibus non tradere mores.[58]

Minus gaudent qui timuere nihil.[59]

It is often some Epicurean ideal of life that he proclaims.

Tomorrow I will live, the Fool does say;
To Day itself's too late; the Wise liv'd Yesterday.[60]

Cowley translates the epigram ending with this
apothegm; Herrick paraphrases it; Mackenzie
quotes part of it as a motto for a copy of the
Lounger; Jeremy Taylor embodies it in a sermon. It seems to be the source of a passage in
Young's *Night Thoughts* and at least has its
likenesses to Shelley's " Where art thou, beloved Tomorrow? " The sentiment, " Tomorrow's life too late is, live today," [61] as Herrick
renders the Latin line, has also been imitated
by many poets from Opitz and Musophilus to
Richard Garnett; and Jeremy Taylor, with his
genius for making Scripture quote the devil,
applies the sentiment, in his discourse on *Re-
pentance,* to the pursuit of the religious life.
In his *Hesperides,* Herrick commends to the
world nearly three hundred precepts and moral
panaceas, of which the vast majority are defi-
nitely remembered quite as well as they deserve
to be. Few of Martial's Epicurean utterances
does he fail to include among them, without acknowledgment even when he gives a close
translation:

Let's live in haste, use pleasures while we may:
Could life return, 'twould never lose a day.[62]

Jonson often does likewise. Eat, drink, and be
merry:

He *that but living half his age, dies such*
M*akes the whole longer than 'twas given him,*
    much —

Q*ui sic vel medio finitus vixit in aevo,*
    Longior huic facta est quam data vita fuit.[63]

Dr. Cotton was another of the many good men
who have approved, by use, the epigrammatist's Epicureanism: *Semper de tribus una
secat*[64] — "And of The Three one severs,
ever."

But it is not only in selfish Epicureanism
that Martial shows his power of sententious
phrase. Lord Bacon quotes his,

O *quantum est subitis casibus ingenium* —[65]
H*ow quick a wit in sudden straits is found,*

and in his *Of Counsel* writes: "But the best
remedy is if Princes knew their Counsellors, as
well as their Counsellors know them: *Principis
est virtus maxima, nosse suos*,"[66] a sentiment
echoed by Owen and adapted by Jonson to
King James: "In a Prince it is no little virtue
to know who are his." In his *Observations on
The Art of Painting*, Dryden quotes and amplifies another of Martial's aphorisms: "*Qui sua
metitur pondera ferre potest:*[67] in order that

[84]

we may undertake nothing beyond our forces,
we must endeavour to know them; on this pru-
dence our reputation depends; a man ought to
cultivate those talents that make his genius."

> *With none too intimately live;*
> *Less you'll rejoice, and less will grieve —* [68]

this sentiment too, fortunately refuted, for the
most part, in practice, meets us often in modern life and literature, beginning with Vincent
Bourne's Latin epigram, translated by Cowper.

> *If thou from Fortune dost no servant crave,*
> *Believe me, thou no master need'st to have —* [69]

Cowley's translation of *servom* and *regem* may
seem to give the Latin lines a somewhat special significance for contemporary housewives,
but in its original breadth the sentiment has
been adopted by writers even so different as
Prior and Shenstone; and Addison, in his *Dia-
logue on Medals*, translates another part of the
same epigram.

More frequently used, however, than any of
these dicta is the last distich of the notable
epigram on Antonius Primus, translated so ex-
cellently by Pope — who uses its thought elsewhere in his poems — and translated even bet-

ter by Sir Henry Newbolt, thinks the author of *The Adventure of Living* [70] who quotes Newbolt's version and applies the epigram to his own father. The good man, with nothing to regret, with no unpleasant recollections,

> *he lives twice, who can at once employ*
> *The present well, and ev'n the past enjoy.*[71]

Bourne quotes the lines in one of his epitaphs; Herrick embodies them in one of the *Hesperides;* Cowley adapts the whole epigram in a poem of his own; they furnish the *Spectator, Rambler, Lounger,* and Rogers' *Pleasures of Memory* with a motto, Taylor with a text, and even Colley Cibber with an idea, as the basis of his autobiography.

The 1659 edition of the " Posthumous Poems of Richard Lovelace, Esq." has as its motto:

> *Those honours come too late*
> *That on our ashes wait.*

And the original line, *Cineri gloria sera venit,*[72] is the motto of Jonson's *Underwoods,* and of a copy of the *Connoisseur,* as well, where it receives the interesting translation:

> *Fame to our ashes comes, alas, too late*
> *And praise smells rank upon the coffin plate.*

Taylor's amplification of the thought is, as usual, very generous.

> *Non est vivere, sed valere vita est —*
> *Not who live long, but happily, are old,*[73]

as an anonymous seventeenth-century translator phrases it. This sentiment, also, often meets us later. Johnson and Steele, among others, quote the Latin line, and Herrick more than once adapts it in his distinctions between " living and lasting." " There is more consistency," writes Montaigne, " in suffering the chain we are tied to than in breaking it; and there is more pregnant evidence of fortitude in Regulus than in Cato:

> *Rebus in angustis facile est contemnere vitam;*
> *Fortiter ille facit qui miser esse potest.*[74]

> *The wretched well may laugh at death, but he*
> *Is braver far who lives in misery."*

Taylor also makes use of the distich and it was a favorite with poets of the seventeenth century in Germany. Montaigne and Taylor again are among those who quote the second line of another epigram:

> Ne laudet dignos, laudat Callistratus omnes.
>   Cui malus est nemo, quis bonus esse potest? [75]

This distich gave Carlo Roncalli a quatrain and seems to have been in Campion's mind when he wrote, in his *Observations in the Art of English Poesie*, as *An Example Epigrammaticall:*

> Kind in every kinde,
> This, deare Ned, resolve.
> Never of thy prayse
> Be too prodigall;
> He that prayseth all
> Can praise truly none.

One of the most charming of Martial's little portrayals of the ideal life deserves quotation, in Courthope's translation rather than in Cowley's paraphrase:

> If you and I, my Julius, could
> But spend our leisure as we would,
> And all our holidays employ
> To taste together life's pure joy,
> We should have nought to say at all
> To rich men's feasts and splendid hall,
> Stiff law-suit or the forum's crowd,
> Or effigies of grandsires proud;
> But drives, talks, walks, the Stoic School,
> Books, exercise, the Virgin's Pool,

Warm baths, cool shades, should be life's rule.
Yet neither of us two, alas!
Dares for himself his life to pass:
The good suns, as they die, each day
Stand to our count. One knows the way
To live: to live why then delay? [76]

Materialistic, Epicurean, to be sure, but so very humanly and decently materialistic! No wonder that good Dr. Cotton did not shudder to pick a title for a poem of his own from such Epicureanism — that famous sun-dial favorite, *Pereunt et Imputantur*. No wonder, either, that the worldly author of *The Man of Feeling* could pick a motto from the same epigram. Such an expression of camaraderie, combined with that really fine thought in another epigram — though a thought perhaps taken by Martial from Seneca as it certainly was later taken from Martial by Johnson —

Who gives to friends, so much from Fate secures,
That is the only wealth for ever yours, [77]

goes far toward explaining Martial's place in the esteem of those he loved.

Fortuna multis dat nimis, satis nulli —

Fortune, they say, doth give too much to many;
But yet she never gave enough to any, [78]

[89]

as Sir John Harington's translation runs. Owen, Wernicke, Weckherlin, and Logau were other early imitators of this epigram.

Inferior matrona suo sit, Prisce, marito;
  Non aliter fiunt femina virque pares.

Let matrons to their heads inferior be,
Else man and wife have no equality.[79]

            Quoiq' il en puisse estre
Je ne suis point si sot que d' épouser non maistre,

says Boileau; and even in this advanced, and advancing, day the opinion finds some muttered support.

  That there's no God, John gravely swears,
  And quotes, in proof, his own affairs;
  For how should such an atheist thrive,
  If there was any God alive?

reads a *Westminster Review* version of another epigram,[80] also appropriated by Harington. It may remind one of Clough's stanza in *Dipsychus,*

  " There is no God," the wicked saith,
    " And truly it's a blessing,
  For what he might have done with us
    It's better only guessing,"

as *Nec minor ista tuae laurea pacis erat* [81] may remind one of Milton's, " Peace hath her victories no less renowned than war." Another line, upon a fool, instead of upon an emperor,

He *who is not wiser than enough, is wise,*[82]

also might remind one, in suspicious mood, of Pope's " The fool is happy that he knows no more," of Heath's *Blessed Ignorance,* and even of Gray's " Where ignorance is bliss, 'tis folly to be wise."

But we return to firmer ground in two more epigrams which must be our last illustrations of the influence of Martial as a moralist and aphorist. The first one, written to Quintilian, with its familiar conclusion,

Enough for me a roof with well-smoked beams,
A garden of wild herbs, and running streams;
My slave content, not very learn'd my wife,
Dreamless my sleep, and without suits my life,[83]

is paraphrased by Cowley, reproduced by Herrick, gives matter for discussion to Dr. Johnson, and is adapted to religious purposes by Taylor. The second is the famous

Vitam quae faciant beatiorem,[84]

[91]

Courthope's version of which has already been quoted. Any man who could write in serious vein a thirteen-line poem which has been translated by Cowley, Fanshawe, Fenton, Fletcher, Somerville, and Surrey, imitated, in whole or part, by Acidalius and by several other Latin epigrammatists, by Weckherlin and a dozen other German epigrammatists, by Ronsard, Herrick, Pope, and Bishop Corbet; which has been quoted by Dryden, Jonson, Racine, Thomas Warton, Montaigne and Martin Luther; which has provided a motto for the *Rambler,* given Taylor a sermon, Bacon and Johnson a subject for discussion, served as a religious tract in sixteenth-century Germany, and come down even into the *Biglow Papers* — such a man surely cannot be disposed of as merely a cynical satirist of debasing influence.

As Herrick is unique among English poets, so is Martial unique among ancient poets in the frequency of his expressions of admiration, affection, and solicitude for his verses, his fame, and for his literary friends. Each of the two has left nearly one hundred and fifty poems on these themes, and Herrick clearly imitates his predecessor in very many of them. But Her-

rick has not been alone in enjoying the epigrammatist's interest in his books and in the
friends who like them and can appreciate them.
The epigram [85] in which Martial warns his
volume against the " rhinocerote's nose," as
Jonson gives it, the superciliousness of Mistress Rome, where, in the midst of " Bravos! "
you are apt to be shot heavenward in a
blanket —

> *Ibis ab excussó missus in astra sagó,*

as the Etonians used to shout the line when
they tossed their victims high — is one of many
which have often been imitated. Fielding
quotes and translates a couple of lines from
it:

> *No town can such a gang of critics show,*
> *Even boys turn up that nose they cannot blow,*

and the motto of his comedy, *The Intriguing
Chambermaid, Majores nusquam rhonchi,* is
taken from the same two lines. Weckherlin,
Logau, and a number of other writers give us
this epigram in German; it appears in the
French of Ronsard; Boileau prefaces his
Epistle à mes Vers with a quotation from it,
and sends his own ambitious book out into the

world with much the same admonitions as
Martial's; Herrick renders the last two lines,

Whither, mad maiden, wilt thou roam?
Far safer 'twere to stay at home;

and *Poteras tutior esse domi* gives Vincent
Bourne a title.

More pleasant, more modest, and more imitated are the epigrams which Martial writes to
friends whose smile or frown can raise a poet
or dash him to the ground, whose favorable
verdict will be final. Let his book please the
learned Apollinaris, if it would be approved by
Attic ears, avoid the sneers of envy, and escape
fish dealer or schoolboy in need of wrapping or
of copy paper. Montaigne quotes this poem,[86]
expressing like fears; and Pope, commenting
on Dryden's *Virgil*, refers to " Attic ears " and
to the *aurem Batavam* [87] of another epigram
with the justified remark: " I think I have
brought in two phrases of Martial here very
dexterously." Even Milton apparently remembered the " mackerel wrapping " of either his
Catullus or his Martial in his Latin diatribe
against Claudius Salmasius. In similar vein
Martial begs Severus [88] to revise the book he
sends him: it will then owe more to Severus

than to himself and live for ever — a compliment borrowed by Herrick, and seemingly by Pope, who makes Buckingham its beneficiary. Another new booklet goes to Caesius Sabinus [89] who so admires and quotes it that though sent to but one man it will be read to all; still another goes to Faustinus,[90] accompanied by a sponge — one grand erasure, only, can make it passable. Jonson appropriates both these fancies, and Dryden bestows upon the Duke of Northumberland Martial's approval of Silius Italicus who, leaving public life, surrenders his veteran years to the Muses and to Phoebus, and instead of law courts now courts Helicon.[91]

Many principles of composition and of literary criticism, many " hints to young writers," are casually introduced into these epigrams, as one might expect.

Non *hic Centauros, non Gorgonas Harpyiasque*
  Invenies: hominem pagina nostra sapit [92]

has been quoted not only by poets, not only as a motto for *Rambler, Connoisseur,* and *Adventurer,* but in quite unlikely places also. Burton applies the lines to his *Anatomy of Melancholy:*

[95]

No Centaurs here, no Gorgons look to find,
  My subject is of man and human kind;

another passage from the same epigram, similar in thought, is part of the motto of Sir Edward Coke's *First Institute*. The epigrammatist's protest against always attempting to
say the smart thing — say sometimes what is
merely good, or middling, or even bad [93] — is
expanded by Whately in his *Treatise on Rhetoric* and furnishes forth a stanza of *Don Juan*.
Similar statements regarding his own epigrams —

Some good, some bad, some neither one nor t'other,
  Of such material, sir, are books composed, [94]

as two numbers of the *Spectator* translate the
distich; " a book that's equal is a book that's
bad " [95] — have become commonplaces. His
ridicule of " brevity by the bookful," [96] imitated by Lessing; his

Sint Maecenates, non derunt, Flacce, Marones, [97]

which with the aid of Owen, Opitz, Fuller and
other early writers soon became one of the
really well-known Latin lines; his

[96]

When *the rose reigns, when locks with ointment*
    shine
Let *rigid Cato read these lines of mine,*[98]

as Herrick's translation goes, adapted by Wernicke and by other poets, including Jonson at
the close of his dedication of *Every Man Out of
His Humour;* his conception of the function of
satire,

    To *lash the vices, but the persons spare,*[99]

with its uses by Logau and Franck and Jonson
and Dryden; his

    N*os haec novimus esse nihil,*[100]

which gave Steele a motto and Montaigne material for his essay on *Presumption* — the list
of such literary comments is long.

For a poet who introduces a number of striking verbal effects, later to be imitated, such as
beginning each line of a fifteen-line poem with
the same word, *Hermes,*[101] and beginning and
ending each distich of a twelve-line poem with
the same phrase, *rumpitur invidia,*[102] Martial's
remark, quoted by Campion, that " we cultivate a sterner Muse "[103] than the Greeks,
might seem inappropriate. But he is speaking

of rules of quantity. With those poetasters who really took liberties with the language, who introduced really bizarre effects or metrical fantasies he had little patience. He is followed by Addison and Butler in such strictures as

> *Turpe est difficiles habere nugas*
> *Et stultus labor est ineptiarum* — [104]

"How foolish is the toil of trifling cares," as Dr. Johnson puts it; the "hard trifles," "serious follies" of Ben Jonson; or in the somewhat disconcerting translation of Charles Rollin's *Belles Lettres:*

> *The deep and dull researches of the schools*
> *Are but the busy indolence of fools.*

Nor did Martial have much patience with those who loved to drag in strange words, archaisms, ancient roughnesses of style;[105] and here again he is followed by Jonson, in his *Discoveries,* with quotation and comment.

Martial's comments on *Vers Libre* would be stimulating. He himself wore the shackles of metre unconsciously and though he used only some half dozen metrical forms, so not competing with Horace, or even with Catullus, in fitting Latin thoughts to Greek measures, the forms he did use he used with such perfect ease and finality as to make a Scaliger declare his work to be " divine."

" Divine " is an adjective which has seldom been associated with Martial, even as a stylist. But still another large portion of his work is, if not divine, at least very genially and graciously human. His charming little epithalamium [106] for Claudia and Rufus, imitated as early as the time of Ausonius, with its translations and mottoes in *Spectator* and *Rambler*, with its pleasant closing lines, quaintly rendered by Fletcher,

> *May she so love him old, that to him shee*
> *Though old indeed, may not seem so to bee,*

is only one of a number of tiny lyrics, sincere and graceful, in honour of an institution which he enjoyed seeing others enjoy. Of Calenus, for example, happily married now for fifteen years to his Sulpicia, he writes:

> *Those other years as nothing were:*
> *You count your life these years with her.*[107]

Sincere and graceful, too, are the many little poems celebrating some friend's birthday or party or gift or return from abroad, some happy event, some meeting. The opening lines of one such poem,

> I, *felix rosa, mollibusque sertis*
> *Nostri cinge comas Apollinaris,*[108]

led Herrick into one of the prettiest of his love songs,

> *Goe, happy Rose, and enterwove*
> *With other Flowers, bind my love,*

and apparently gave Waller his " Go, lovely Rose." Love for Manius, Martial's boyhood friend, affection for whom draws him back to Spain, a friend with whom he would share any danger, visit any clime, is told, in words that hardly seem a mere echo of Propertius:

> *Feel as I feel, love me as I love you,*
> *And we'll make any spot a Rome, for two.*[109]

The picture of Antonius, " with violets and roses decked," is good, but far better:

> *Ars utinam mores animumque effingere posset!*
> *Pulchrior in terris nulla tabella foret!* [110]

The tribute has come down into lines of Opitz and of other writers, but is best known in

Jonson's verses under the engraving of Shakespeare:

> O *could he but have drawn his wit*
> As *well in brass as he has hit*
> His *face! The print would then surpass*
> All *that was ever writ in brass.*

Over the chimney-piece of Jonson's club room
in the Old Devil Tavern were his *Leges Con-
viviales*, a number of them taken from Martial: *Joci sine felle sunto,*[111] *Neminem reum
pocula faciunto,*[112] " Nor shall our cups make
guilty men," as he translates it in one of his
poems. Jonson, like many another later poet,
cordially approved of the epigrammatist's
pleasant invitations to what must have been
very pleasant dinner parties and frequently
imitated them even in minute details such as in
announced exaggeration of the menu,[113] " I'll
tell you of more and lie, so you will come," or
in some promise to read not one line of his own
verse but let the prospective guest recite whole
epics.[114]

One of Martial's devices, distantly Hora-
tian, is to launch into a long description of
somebody, reserving the name of the person

until the very end. He catalogues a man's virtues and then, finally, declares:

> Dispeream si non hic Decianus erit.[115]

Swift gives us a similar catalogue, and ends:

> Jove mix'd up all and the best clay employ'd;
> Then called the happy composition Floyd.

Jonson uses the same method in his epigram
upon Lucy, Countess of Bedford, Lamb in his
poem on Rotha Quillinan, Piron in his lines
Contre le Poëte Roi. Herrick tells us of girls
whiter than swans, lilies, snow, pearls, ivory,
cream, and moonlight, girls who smell sweeter
than incense, spices, amber, musk, dewy fields,
vineyards, pomegranates, balm, myrrh, nard,
wine, flowers, beehives, phoenix nests. His
sweethearts are Martial's children,[116] in their
complex whiteness and sweetness. In other
poems Herrick exhausts his ingenuity, and his
readers, in naming fragrant things before he
tells us the purport of it all:

> Thus sweet she smells, or what can be
> More lik'd by her or lov'd by me.

We should undoubtedly have been spared the
suspense but for Martial [117] who not only never

spared suspense but at least once, agreeing with the *Tatler's* opinion, " there is no carrying a metaphor too far when a lady's charms are spoken of," let his enthusiasm over the charms of six-year-old Erotion carry him so far that Burton, in Freudian mood, declared such hyperbolical comparisons to be evidence of love-melancholy. Certainly there would be melancholy of some sort in the poet's breast, could he see Burton's version of one distich:

> To *whom confer'd a Peacock's indecent,*
> A *Squirrel harsh, a Phoenix too frequent.*[118]

Luckily this poem, and others like it, have fallen into Spenser's and Jonson's kindlier hands.

> Have *you seen but a bright lily grow*
>   Before *rude hands have touch'd it?*
> Have *you mark'd but the fall of snow*
>   Before *the soil hath smutched it?*
> Have *you felt the wool of the beaver?*
>   Or *swan's down ever?*
> Or *have smelt o' the bud of the brier?*
>   Or *the nard in the fire?*
> Or *have tasted the bag of the bee?*
>   O *so white! O so soft! O so sweet is she!*

It is not often that Martial writes a real love poem. When he does, and succeeds in seeming interested and fervent, he is apt to seem, also, reminiscent of Catullus. Yet even when he turns to this unfamiliar and comparatively unsuccessful theme he has not been without influence.

You ask me, dear friend, "What lass I'd enjoy."
  I would have one that's neither too coming nor
    coy.
A medium is best that gives us no pain,
  By too much indulgence, or too much disdain.[119]

Ausonius, Opitz, and Henry King are among the later poets who directly imitated this epigram, and, combined with a line or two from another epigram,[120]

> *Lucretia toto*
> *Sis licet usque die, Laida nocte volo,*

it seems to have given Herrick his

> *Lucrece all day be,*
> *Thais in the night to me.*
> *Be she such as neither will*
> *Famish me or overfill.*

The epigrammatist's sentiment,

Insequeris, fugio; fugis, insequor; haec mihi mens
    est:
  Velle tuum nolo, Dindyme, nolle volo,[121]

clearly gives epigrams to Politian and Weissenborn, but this particular expression of so common a sentiment probably had nothing to do with such later expressions as Jonson's

> *So court a mistress, she denies you;*
>   *Let her alone, she will court you,*

or Lowell's

> *Coy Hebe flies from those that woo.*

Unquestionably much imitated, however, is the epigram on Cleopatra, who shuns her bridegroom's embrace and plunges into the gleaming pool only to be betrayed by the water through which her body glistens:

> *Condita sic puro numerantur lilia vitro,*
>   *Sic prohibet tenuis gemma latere rosas —* [122]

> As *Lillies shrin'd in Christall, so*
>   Do *thou to me appear;*
> Or *Damask Roses when they grow*
>   To *sweet acquaintance there,*

writes Herrick. And again, combining these lines of Martial with a couple of others,

Femineum lucet sic per bombycina corpus,
Calculus in nitida sic numeratur aqua,[123]

Herrick gives us:

So *Lillies thorough Christall look:*
So *purest pebbles in the brook:*
As *in the River Julia did,*
Halfe *with a lawne of water hid.*

Steele translates the epigram and remarks upon it in the *Spectator;* Prior's Phillis, in his *Non-pareil,* is similarly described. Thomson, in *The Seasons,* tells of another lady bathing, one September morn,

As *shines the lily through the crystal mild*
Or *as the rose amid the morning dew;*

even Thomas Flatman uses the simile in an effusion winsomely entitled *On Mrs. E. Montague's Blushing in the Cross-bath.*

Nolueram, Polytime, tuos violare capillos[124] gave Pope his motto for *The Rape of the Lock.* The epigram beginning, *Laevia sex cyathis, septem Justina bibatur,*[125] is quoted by Voltaire and among the imitations of it is Dr. Nash's,

> To *every letter drink a glass*
> *That fills the name you fancy.*
> *Take four if Suky be your lass,*
> *And five, if it be Nancy.*

Steele, telling of the Amorous Club at Oxford, refers to this epigram, and continues: " A young student who is in love with Miss Elizabeth Dimple, was so unreasonable as to begin her health under the name of Elizabeth, which so exasperated the Club, that, by common consent, we retrenched it to ' Betty '." Martial was apparently free from any such restrictions: on one occasion, if his girl does not appear, he proposes to drink the full name of Instantius Rufus.[126]

In neither the lady nor the liquor would the poet have found any profound interest. There were too many other things in life for him. Even his power of turning a pretty speech was usually reserved for his male, rather than female, friends, and for his emperors:

Moribus hic vivat principis, ille suis — [127]
Live Senate as our ruler lives, he as he does;

Dux tibi sit semper talis, et iste diu — [128]
Mayst thou have ever such a Chief, and this Chief
    long;

Si Cato reddatur, Caesarianus erit — [129]
Cato, returned, would be our Caesar's man.

Sometimes his emperors deserved encomiums,
as did Nerva these. But deserved or not, it is
not infrequently that the epigrammatist's compliments have served the loyalty of later bards.
Jonson's motto for his panegyric on James is
Licet toto nunc Helicone frui.[130] In his *Devices,*
and elsewhere, he translates Martial's words to
Titus, " He meets not to offend, that hastes to
please." [131] *Par domus est caelo, sed minor est
domino,*[132] has gratified many a monarch since
Domitian's day, including Louis the Fourteenth, and

> *I am, Caesar, vel nocte veni: stent astra licebit,*
>   *Non derit populo te veniente dies* [133]

was re-born for neither the first nor last time
in Cowley's,

When you appear, Great Prince, our night is done.

Addison quotes and translates part of the epigram in which Martial bids Flattery go to
Parthia, now that Trajan has arrived and
brought back rustic Truth.[134] Even Milton's
picture of ancient Rome, sketched by the
Tempter in *Paradise Regained,* may have been

suggested not only by Juvenal, but also by the epigrammatist's description of the vast city to which flock men of every race and hue and speech who yet unite in acclaiming their Caesar " Father of his Country." [135]

Martial, of course, was primarily an urban poet, an observer of life in a great metropolis. No account of his influence would be complete which failed to emphasize the fact that a tremendous amount of plain information is given by his epigrams to archaeologist and topographer, historian and essayist. Emerson, in saying that Martial will give the reader " Roman manners — and some very bad ones — in the early days of the Empire," was quite right, if somewhat wrong in recommending him as one of *four* Latin writers to be read. Even the *Liber Spectaculorum*, the *Xenia*, and the *Apophoreta*, have been invaluable to scholars. Yet the *Book of the Games* has had some literary influence, too. Rabelais, for example, quotes Leander's cry,

Parcite dum propero, mergite cum redeo,[136]

as he breasts the waters of the Hellespont to meet his Hero. Voltaire too admired the epigram and its French translation:

Léandre conduit par l'amour
En nageant, disoit aux orages,
Laissez moi gagner tes rivages,
Ne me noyez qu' à mon rétour.

Burton, by the way, this time more plausibly, cites the cry as a strong symptom of love-melancholy.

But in the other twelve books there are so many charming occasional poems, on the sights, the contents, the doings of that ancient world, that some critics go so far as to declare that Martial is "most enjoyable when he is least epigrammatic." Here is a distich on some picture or statue,[137] to be imitated by Lessing; here a few lines on a bee or an ant, caught and enshrined in a glorious amber tomb,[138] to appear again in the verse of Cunradinus, Opitz, Tickell, Lovelace, Pope, Herrick, Montgomery, even in what is at the present moment the last novel of Rupert Hughes; here a comment, to be picked up by Addison, on dry Ravenna where a cistern was more precious than a vineyard;[139] here a little poem on a fragment of the Argo,[140] which Cowley kept in mind. Street scenes, temples, shops, baths, colonnades, theatres, dead dogs, live lions — the list is long

and various. One description of the bustling
city may be quoted in full:

Why am I brought so oft, and by what charm,
To dry Nomentum and this humble farm?
For poor men, Sparsus, who would find a space
For sleep and thinking, Rome affords no place.
You claim to live; but all deny your right,
By morn schoolmasters, bakers' men by night;
Armies of copper-smiths, a thousand strong,
Go hammer, hammer, hammer all day long.
Your money-changers here, a lazy horde,
Rattle gold coins upon their dirty board;
There ponderous mallets, pounding Spanish rock
For lumps of gold, the midnight chamber shock.
Add to the noise Bellona's drunken crew,
The shipwrecked mariner, the begging Jew,
Ay, and blind beggars, selling matches, too!
He, who can tell how many clamours keep
The weary Roman from his noonday sleep,
Can count the brazen instruments as soon
Of those who beat their gongs to help the moon.
You, Sparsus, of these plagues can nothing tell,
Who, far-removed, in dainty villa dwell,
And on the slumbering hills look down at home,
To see your farm and vineyard both in Rome.
Your grapes are large as what Falernum stores;
Your house so spacious you may drive indoors;

[111]

No *noise breaks in upon your sleep at night;*
By *day nought wakes you but admitted light.*
For *me the laughter of the passing crowd,*
All *Rome beneath my bedroom, shrill and loud,*
Disgust *me ever with some fresh alarm:*
Hence, *when I wish to sleep, I seek this farm.*[140a]

In Jonson's *The Silent Woman* a similar collection of street noises annoys Morose; and
Boileau, in his poem on the noises of Paris, also
seems to remember Martial, whose familiar
phrase, *rus in urbe,* he laboriously paraphrases, "sans sortie de la ville, il trouve la
campagne."

Urban poet though he primarily was, Martial never tires of extolling the carefree country life of Italy and Spain, the cool summer
villas of his friends, the seaside and mountain
resorts of the ancient world. His long fifty-one
line epigram,[141] telling of the practical, worka-
day farm of the open-handed Faustinus, might
almost as well be called a pastoral. Like others
of these rural pieces, it contains much that later
generations have appropriated. It gave Jonson
many a suggestion for his *Penshurst* and Herrick for his *Panegerick to Sir Lewis Pemberton,*
of whose liberal table he heartily approves;

[112]

Pope alludes to Faustinus' country-seat and
paraphrases several lines, among them:

> But *simpler Nature's hand with nobler grace,*
> *Diffuses artless beauties o'er the place;*

Bishop Hall imitates the poem; the *Connois-*
seur quotes and translates the last five lines,
which give an epigrammatic conclusion to the
pastoral by contrasting this real farm with
Bassus' suburban villa that produces merely
" starvation, in style " —

> 'T*is not the country, you must own,*
> 'T*is only London out of town.*

Cowley is only one of a number of poets who
have found almost more to admire and imitate
in these pastoral epigrams [142] than in any other
part of Martial's work, abounding as they do
in felicitous touches of description — *viva*
quies ponti,[143] " such a tide as moving seems
asleep " — full as they are of genuine love of
countryside beauty, of rural sports, of his own
little estate that he would not exchange for the
possessions of an Alcinous. The satirist is lost
in the idyllist. One may understand how Horace Walpole could ask a friend if some verses
of the *Georgics* were " not just like Martial."

It should be evident that the epigrammatist was much more than a cynical wit, coarse-grained, heavy-handed, brutal, whose devotion to the epigram debased it only. He sincerely admired the good things in literature that were within his range of vision and seemed to him real — Catullus' downrightness, Ovid's brilliance, Seneca's nobility, Virgil's fitness, Greek daintiness. He borrowed freely, too, from the dead poets whom he admired, but usually contrived to make such borrowings his own. Yet the moods and themes, the character and aspirations, the spiritual insight and aesthetic sensitiveness of many of his predecessors were beyond him. Had not this been so, we of course should not have had our Martial. Pope is not Shelley, and, on the whole, it is just as well. Martial is not Lucretius — luckily we have them both. But this fact, at least, let us repeat, should be clear, that, though he was an observer rather than a thinker, a realist rather than an idealist, a stylist rather than a seer, much of his work is not without thoughtfulness, not without fineness of feeling, not without beauty; and it should be equally clear that much of his influence upon later writers has been quite outside the realm of pungent wit.

But it is as a wit, of course, that he has been most widely known, most influential. His Rome was, after all, so like — so pitifully like, a Heracleitus would feel — our London, Paris, Berlin, New York; his people and the situations into which they get are, after all, so close to our people and our situations. A somewhat larger proportion of our own jokes, perhaps, are made at the expense of a rather nicer sort of person than Martial generally chooses to laugh at, and we may therefore feel that our own wit is better-tempered than his. Many of the most amusing things in Dickens, for instance, are the eccentricities or defects of good and lovable people. Few of Martial's butts, except himself, are persons with whom we should like to live. The really good man or woman he seldom makes fun of, even pleasantly. Fabianus [144] is told, in kindly, laudatory fashion carried on by Cowley, that Rome is no place for him, one who will not be " Buffoon nor Bawd," " nor Bribe nor Flatter any of the Great." No doubt Fabianus had certain traits which might have been made laughable. But Martial did not choose to get his laugh that way. Quite another person suffers by the point of the epigram.

To be sure, he cannot always refrain from a gentle poke at some very strait-laced worthy: Safronius,[145] for instance, so modest in mind and aspect — how *could* he have managed to become a father? And Fabullinus [146] who, like Lamb's gentleman " of incorrigible and losing honesty," is constantly imposed upon — but then, many a good man remains a tyro. Ordinarily, to Martial, Cato is the stalwart moral Cato of legend and history to whom he often refers with at least remote respect in lines [147] like those of Pope's:

> *Such plays alone should win a British ear*
> *As Cato's self had not disdained to hear.*

Yet he does falter in that faith and feel that Cato was possibly unco guid on that notable occasion when he stalked into the theatre, knowing well that the licentious *Floralia* were on, and at once stalked out. As Addison translates it:

> *With awful countenance and brow severe,*
> *What in the name of goodness dost thou here?*
> *See the mixt crowd! How giddy, lewd, and vain!*
> *Didst thou come in but to go out again?* [148]

No, the people whom Martial ridiculed generally deserved ridicule at the very least, and

frequently deserved hanging; it is this fact
largely that accounts for a comparative lack
of amiableness in the epigrammatist's wit, a
far greater inclination to laugh at than with
his victims. Naturally, there are a number who,
apart from their idiosyncrasies, are apparently
decent citizens enough, and are treated more or
less gently. Some of his lovers are in this number. There is Quintus, for example, Lessing's
Sextus:

" *Quintus loves Thais.*" " *What Thais is that?* "
  " *Why, Thais the one-eyed, who* " — " *Who?*
Well, I was aware she lost one of her pair,
    But Quintus, it seems, has lost two." [149]

Or there is Rufus,[150] whom Wernicke introduces to the Germans and Steele to the English:

  Let Rufus weep, rejoice, stand, sit, or walk,
  Still he can nothing but of Naevia talk;
  Let him eat, drink, ask questions, or dispute,
  Still he must speak of Naevia or be mute.
  He writ to his father, ending with this line:
"I *am, my lovely Naevia, ever thine.*"

Nor is Galla [151] treated roughly, perjured
though she be. Galla is like Thomas Freeman's
Cloe:

> For *when thou swear'st, thou liest, I know:*
> D*ost hate me, Cloe? Prythee swear,*
> For *then I know thou lov'st me dear.*

Martial himself, however, has a Chloe [152] whom he does treat roughly, incidentally leading Thomas Moore to allege that he also could resign that eye of blue, that roseate cheek, that snowy neck, and those sweet lips:

> I*n short, so well I've learned to fast,*
>   T*hat, sooth my love, I know not whether*
> I *might not bring myself at last*
>   T*o — do without you altogether.*

Gentleness is not entirely absent even in the case of Priscus and Paula, though the lady pays for it:

> Y*ou wish to marry Priscus, Paula?*
>   V*ery wise of you!*
> P*riscus, though, declines, you tell me?*
>   H*e's wise, too.*[153]

Priscus and Paula have had many descendants, Taburot's and Leigh Hunt's pairs among them:

> A*bel fain would marry Mabel;*
>   W*ell, it's very wise of Abel;*
> B*ut Mabel won't at all have Abel;*
>   W*ell, it's wiser still of Mabel.*

Priscus is rather a good sort, on the whole, and is gently treated, too, in his rôle of statistical psychologist. Dr. Johnson, who translates the epigram, was interested in Martial's reaction:

Priscus: you've often asked me how I'd live
Should Fate at once both wealth and honour give?
What soul his future conduct can foresee?
Tell me what sort of lion you would be.[154]

Even Linus, in the most attractive of his rôles, that of general nuisance, is laughed at without really undue savageness:

You ask what I grow on my Sabine estate.
  Well, Linus, this answer is true:
I grow on that soil, far from urban turmoil —
  Very happy at not seeing you.[155]

Lessing gives us a nameless Linus:

" Was nutzt dir nun dein ferner Garten? He? "
  Dass ich dich dort nicht seh!

But regardless of the treatment accorded them by Martial, whether genial or truculent, let us survey some of his acquaintances, not unknown to modern writers and the modern world. There is the dilettante Atticus,[156] for example, who does this, that, and the other thing prettily, but nothing well. Atticus is somewhat like Juvenal's Greekling and Dryden's Zimri, "mankind's epitome," still more like Ugo Foscolo's Lampredi, and entirely like one of Logau's butts. Logau was well acquainted, too, with one of Atticus' kinsmen, Laurus,[157] so sicklied o'er by the pale cast of thought that he cannot determine what career to follow. Mark Twain would have ascribed a prodigious quantity of mind to Laurus: it takes him so long to make it up.

> *Old Priam's age, or Nestor's may be out*
> *And thou, O Taurus, still go on in doubt,*

as Dr. Johnson translates it. Hurry up, choose your vocation:

> *On any one amiss thou canst not fall;*
> *Thou'lt end in nothing if thou grasp'st at all,*

as Sedley continues it, or, as it might be phrased:

> *Come, end your hesitation, end your thought,*
> *Or you and your career will end in nought.*

Still another of Martial's ne'er-do-wells, Sertorius,[158] is adopted by Logau. Sertorius is in quite as bad case as Laurus: he begins all sorts of things, but always comes to some lame and impotent conclusion. He is Lessing's Rufinus, but slightly refined:

Rufinus endet nichts, er fängt nur alles an.
Ob alles? Lesbia, sprich doch! Du kennst den
*   Mann.*

Also Logau's, as well as Homburg's and Grob's, is Martial's busybody, Olus,[159] who pokes into this person's morals — *Ole, quid ad te?* — or into that person's debts — *Ole, quid ad te?* — yet ignores his own fading credit — *hoc ad te pertinet, Ole* — and his own wife's wayward-ness — *hoc ad te pertinet, Ole.* Martial could mention scores of other things that do pertain to Olus, but rightly concludes, *Sed quid agas ad me pertinet, Ole, nihil.*

More engaging than Olus is Martial's friend of moody nature whom Pope quotes to Swift and whose traits Addison amplifies:

In all thy humours, whether grave or mellow,
Thou'rt such a touchy, testy, pleasant fellow,
Hast so much wit and mirth and spleen about thee,
There is no living with thee, or without thee.[160]

Prior's grievous condition seems to have been due to the same sort of person —

Wretched when from thee, vexed when nigh,
I with thee or without thee die —

known also, of course, to Ovid. Without even
intervals of agreeableness, however, is Sabidius.[161] Sabidius appears in many modern epigrammatists, including Marot, Weckherlin,
and Lessing, but it is Tom Brown " of facetious
memory " who ensured his immortality. Sum-
moned by his College Dean, Dr. Fell, so the
story goes, and in danger of being sent down
because of consistent idleness and misbehav-
iour, Brown was given one final chance to show
his worth. Opening a volume of Martial at ran-
dom the Dean told Brown to translate. The
lines were:

Non amo te, Sabidi, nec possum dicere quare:
Hoc tantum possum dicere, non amo te.

Instantly Brown rendered them:

    I *do not love thee, Doctor Fell.*
    T*he reason why I cannot tell.*
    B*ut this alone I know full well,*
    I *do not love thee, Doctor Fell.*

The effect was successful. Brown stayed in
Christ Church and Sabidius vicariously entered
Parliament, at least in a speech of Sheridan's,

and into the knowledge of thousands of readers unacquainted with the classics, the world over.

Martial's professional men, and their modern successors, might furnish material for a separate chapter. There is Naevolus,[162] later to be Herrick's orator, who can find words only when the House is in an uproar. " Now! Now it's quiet! Now for your oration! " Stillness audible continues. Here are the school-teachers, " detested by girls and by boys," their early lessons and raucous lectures equally detested by the epigrammatist:

We *next door wish to doze during some of the night*
    hours:
    Entire lack of sleep makes us ill.
Let *'em out! What they pay you for bawling,*
    We'll pay, if you only keep still.[163]

One " ferule-sceptred " pedagogue is adjured to be easy on his tender flock, the last line of the adjuration being the famous

Aestate pueri si valent, satis discunt.[164]

And the lawyers! Here is Cinna [165] who needs ten hours to say nine words. Oh, silence eloquent, profound! Or there is Pannychus, who has abandoned his legal career, " The small but sure reward of threadbare gown," as the *Spectator* translates it, to become a farmer:

But your practice at law was a farm hard to beat,
  Though your fees did occasion some banter.
As a lawyer you sold the beans, barley, and wheat
  That you now have to buy as a planter.[166]

And Postumus [166a] — Postumus speaks long and fervently upon every topic under the sun, except one in any way related to the case on the docket, the theft of those three goats. Dr. Parr, in his *Bellenden* attacks Pitt as a later Postumus who lays every mishap to Lord North and the war with America. *Deos hominesque testatur bellum Americanum in causa fuisse cur Titius tres capellas a Caio furatus sit.*

But doctors have always been better game than lawyers.

> *Diaulus left his doctoring*
> *To practice undertaking.*
> *His training as a medic, though,*
> *Has really been his making.*[167]

Anselmus, himself a physician of Parma, was one of the first imitators of this epigram, and

was followed by Boileau and many others.
Then there is that Aesculapian of whom Sir
Thomas More also tells:

Though a soldier at present, a doctor of yore,
You but do with a sword what your pills did be-
fore.[168]

It took some medicine, or at least a call, for
most of Martial's medical practitioners to kill.
His Hermocrates,[169] however, whom Montaigne
mentions in telling a series of jokes on the
fraternity, was far more lethal than the rest.
Prior asserts, " I died last night of my physician." But Andragoras, in perfect health all
day, died of seeing Hermocrates merely in a
dream.

Worse than the bad doctor was the bad man
of letters. There seem to have been many of
them at large in Rome. A particularly unfortunate element of the situation was that a literary aspirant in those days gave *recitationes,*
readings, to which his acquaintances were invited, and they were expected to attend. Martial had less patience with the system than did
Pliny who made himself a sufficiently tiresome
part of it. He tells Mamercus:

You recite to us none of your verse,
  Yet wish us to think that you write.
We will gladly think that — or anything else —
  Provided you never recite.[170]

Martial is rather captious, however. Laberius [171] alleges that he can write elegant poems: show us some, then. Varus,[172] on the other hand, writes hundreds of verses daily, but doesn't recite any: he's both wise and foolish, like Lessing's Cytharist, and somewhat like Swift's Arthur:

Arthur, they say, has wit; for what?
For writing? No, for writing not.

It was not necessary for a man to hire a hall and give a formal recitation in order to make himself obnoxious. Ligurinus,[173] later to become Calvelli's poetaster, " occasions a rout whenever he's out; " a good man, like Pope's friend, " without one sin, but poetry," he yet is feared worse than snake, tiger or scorpion just for being *nimis poeta* — a phrase that Dryden and Sir John Denham and Jeremy Taylor find useful. Or there is Theodorus [174] who does his deadly work by book rather than by recitation. Why does he not receive a complimentary

copy of Martial's last volume, he wonders. " I
fear you would send me your own," says Martial, inspiring Marot and Lessing in similar
contingencies. Theodorus' [174a] house burned
down. What an insult to the Muses! Merely
the house? Why not its poetic owner, too? He
would have been the better for a little fire.

> *Cinna writes verses*
>   *Against me, 'tis said.*
> *But no one writes verses*
>   *Whose verse is not read.*[175]

In how many forms this meets us later, from
the frank imitations of a La Martinière or
Hagedorn or Martini or Lessing —

> *Wer sagt, dass Meister Kauz Satiren auf mich*
>   *schreibt?*
> *Wer nennt geschrieben das, was ungelesen bleibt?*

— to the more distant resemblance in Prior's
reflection that in order to find out if he
were really maligned he would have to read
the poet who was said to have maligned him, so
let it pass. Even Coleridge's Zoilus, abducted
by him from George Buchanan or from Carlo
Roncalli, may possibly be related to Martial's
Cinna, as well as to Martial's Zoilus:

In *vain I praise thee, Zoilus!*
In *vain thou rail'st at me!*
Me *no one credits, Zoilus!*
And *no one credits thee.*

Or there is Tucca,[176] Jonson's *Weak Gamester in Poetry,* who pursues Martial into every field of composition, epic, tragedy, lyric, satire, elegy, even epigram:

Choose *some form of writing*
You *find uninviting,*
And *leave it for me to essay.*

Cerrinius,[177] however, is of a different mould, Martial affects to believe. Able to write better epigrams than Martial, he yet refrains:

Land, *gold, and trifles many give or lend,*
But *he that stoops in fame is a rare friend,*

as Jeremy Taylor translates the last two lines. Dryden more than once uses this epigram as a point of departure, and taking the last distich seriously in his *Essay on Satire,* he quotes it and applies it to Dorset, saying with rather more courtliness than candour: " This same prevalence of genius is in your lordship." Watts, also, seriously ascribing the virtue to Dr. Hort, writes:

Rarely a Virgil, a Cirine, we meet,
Who lays his laurels at inferior feet,
And yields the tenderest point of honour, wit.

Bad poets were bad enough, but plagiarists were still more evil. Cordova is warned to suppress that versifier of hers who prigs Martial's epigrams. If the fellow could only write decently himself, Martial would not mind: he could return the compliment in kind. But

A bachelor calmly may flirt with your wife;
A blind man may put out your eyes;
There is nothing much worse than a penniless thief,
Nothing safer than bards you despise.[178]

Dryden is one of many who have lamented with Martial: " These men write that which no man else would steal." And Paulus —

Paulus buys a book of verse,
And reads us then his own:
One's claim, of course, to what one buys
Can legally be shown! [179]

Paulus is Boileau's Abbé Roquette. But Fidentinus [180] is Martial's arch plagiarist. His one original page, in a volume otherwise Martial's, stands out like a crow among swans, a magpie among nightingales. So a poet may be made by

borrowing verses, eh? [181] In that way Aegle
has teeth, though her dentist made them; in
that way swart Lycoris is a blonde, though
white lead did it; in the way you're poetical
now, you'll be curly-headed, when bald. One is
reminded of Byron's lines from Lebrun:

Aegle, beauty and poet, has two little crimes;
She makes her own face and does not make her
rhymes.

Fidentinus appears once with quite notorious
results:

I *wrote that book you read us, as can readily be*
shown;
Y*ou read it, though, so vilely it begins to be your*
own.[182]

Among the imitations of the whole epigram is
Bettinelli's,

E *ver, son miei que' versi:*
M*a da te recitati*
M*i parver sì diversi*
C*he tuoi li ho reputati.*

But the second line in itself has performed
many an office, from giving the *Spectator* a
motto to giving Bishop Latimer his defence of

a sermon wrongly reported. It may very well
have been in Boileau's mind when he answered
his own celebrated inquiry of Perrault as to
why Cicero and Plato, Virgil and Homer
seemed, in Perrault's translations, to be such
utter idiots:

> 'Tis *your inanity, your words,*
> *Your style that makes them so.*
> *You take a towering genius*
> *And make him seem Perrault.*

Last, but not least objectionable, of the men
of letters are the idle, irresponsible reviewers.
Laelius is one of them:

> *You damn every poem I write,*
> *Yet publish not one of your own.*
> *Now kindly let yours see the light,*
> *Or else leave my damned ones alone.*[183]

Corvinus, Herrick, Opitz, Franck, and, audibly
or inaudibly, most other poets have offered
critics the same alternative, and even Sir Edward Coke closes the Preface of his *Reports*
with the Latin lines. Martial, too, like Herrick,
has his critics who will not be convinced that
all mistakes and infelicities are " printers'
errors." [184] " Your epigrams are very distinctly
bad." " So they are. And yours? " Or there is

[131]

that other critic,[185] quoted by Jonson at the
end of *Cynthia's Revels,* who turns red and
white, stands stupefied, gapes and glares when
Martial is praised. " Good enough! Now I
know I am a success." Or here is Chrestillus [186]
who loves the rough archaisms of the old poets,
dotes on phrases like " frugiferous terrene."
Jonson and Watts are among the modern
writers who allude unflatteringly to the taste
of Chrestillus. And there is the critic who has
no use for the dainty, eulogistic epigram, who
wants nothing but gall and wormwood.[187] He
would rather " gnaw a rib than eat the loin of
a Laurentian boar." " All right, drink Vatican,
if you fancy vinegar; my flask was not meant
for folks like you." Logau has a great deal to
say about critics of this type, as does Jonson.
" It is not my fault," says the latter, quoting
from this epigram, " if I fill them out nectar,
and they run to metheglin."

Critics appear everywhere, even in the
" cracker-mottoes," the *Xenia* and *Apophoreta,*
where one of them is told, in Robert Burton's
version,

Wer'st thou all scoffs and flouts, a very Momus,
Than we ourselves thou canst not say worse of
    us.[188]

[132]

Martial's modesty is more to be commended than the anatomy of Burton's melancholy metrics. Sir John Harington is a little happier in his translation of the epigrammatist's better known remark about certain other critics:

The readers and the hearers like my books,
  And yet some writers cannot them digest;
But what care I? for when I make a feast,
  I *would my guests should praise it, not the cooks.*[189]

Congreve, in his *Epilogue* to *Oroonoko*, writes:

Critics, he knows, for this may damn his books:
But he makes feasts for friends and not for cooks.

Bacon quotes the epigram in his *Advancement of Learning*; we come upon it again and again, whether in the Latin of a Posthius, or in the German of a Tscherning. Better known still is the epigram on Vacerra who admires only dead poets. Vacerra is bluntly told:

tanti
Non est, ut placeam tibi, perire.[190]

The sentiment has lingered in many an expected, and unexpected, quarter. We are not

[133]

surprised to find it in Cordus and Paschasius, in Owen, Scherffer, Opitz, Rist or Corvinus, in Cowley and Herrick, in Lessing and Rabutin, in Byron and Samuel Bishop; but it is surprising to find Taylor using it as a text, to find Fuller quoting and translating it in the Preface to his *Worthies,* and remarking: " All men being like-minded with Martial herein, none surviving will distaste their omission in a work confined to the memories of the departed."

But leaving professional men, we observe still more members of that long procession of ancient butts whose heirs are very much alive. The married couples who learn too late that their union was established in other than celestial regions — Martial knew many of them. That pair of his, for instance, later to become Jonson's Giles and Joan, Herrick's Jolly and Jilly, of whom Relph tells us in his translation:

> *Alike in temper and in life,*
> *The crossest husband, crossest wife:*
> *It looks exceedingly odd to me*
> *This well-matched pair can disagree.*[191]

Or Martial's own alleged situation:

I *hear that Lycoris has buried*
Every friend she has had in her life.
I *sincerely regret, Fabianus,*
S*he is not on good terms with my wife.*[192]

Old Bishop Balthasar Bonifacius probably
thought of Martial when he wrote:

All those I love die young: Zoilus, I'll try
To love you, though I loathe you, so you'll die.

Then along comes the censorious Tongilianus,[193] Herrick's Coone, Tongilianus, not
merely long-nosed but *all* nose, a figure common in Logau and in other modern epigrammatists. Smith, writing in the *Tin Trumpet* on
" Bulls," says he omits Irish bulls " upon the
principle that determined Martial not to describe the nose of Tongilianus, because *nil*
praeter nasum Tongilianus habet." Close to
Tongilianus is the fastidious Mamercus,[194]
whom nobody pleases, who *robiginosis cuncta*
dentibus rodit, whom Fielding quotes and discusses, whom Jonson alludes to — " show your
' rusty teeth ' at every word and help to damn
the author."

Seems he satirical to you at worst?
I *think that man, whom none can please, is cursed.*

One recollects La Rochefoucauld's remark: "A man to whom no one is pleasing is much more unhappy than one who pleases nobody." Mamercus still sneers and gnaws in the Latin of Owen, the German of Logau, the Italian of Roncalli. And here is a pompous lawyer,[195] with trains of clerks and loads of briefs, who, for all his learning, all his state, is quite unacquainted with even such simple phrases as "Comment allez-vous" or plain "How do do." If you doubt me, just bid him good day — the snob! Novius,[196] Swift's Old Hunks, who lives next door to Martial, with whom he might shake hands by reaching out from his window, is perhaps not a snob, but for all social purposes Martial feels that he might as well live in Egypt.

> *What correspondence can I hold with you,*
> *Who are so near, and yet so distant too?*

> *Thus he who would not see old Roger,*
> *Must be his neighbour — or his lodger,*

to give both the *Spectator's* paraphrase and Swift's translation of a few lines.

Then the parvenus and braggarts pass by, the fops and ladies' men. Here is Zoilus, rich,

stingy, lecherous, so vicious as to be, like Wernicke's Cleant, not vicious but vice itself.
Zoilus formerly had been a runaway slave, a
fact of which Martial occasionally reminds
him:

The gem in your ring is quite lost in the gold,
  Though the gem is as large as an egg.
A ring of the weight that you wear on your hand
  Would have done very well on your leg.[197]

One of Zoilus' vanities is to get sick in order
to show off his fine bed clothes. In order to get
well, take mine, says Martial.[198] Bishop Hall
was one of the early admirers of Zoilus:

When Zoylus was sicke, he knew not where,
Save his wrought night-cap, and lawn pillow-beer.
Kind fooles! They made him sick that made him
    fine;
Take them away and there's his medicine.

Sir John Davies' Brunus who

    was sick to show his night-cap fine,
  And his wrought pillow overspread with lawn,

Maynard's Anthoine who feigns sickness to
show off his house and its appointments, Mas-
singer's Lady Frugal and her daughter, seem to

be among his next of kin. Or here is Chari-
nus [199] who claims that all his silver is the
handiwork of Mentor, or Myron, or Praxiteles,
or Phidias. Odd Sterling's name — or the
equivalent — is not included, says Martial.
And there is Maximus with his houses in every
quarter of the city. Where is one to call upon
him, anyhow? *Quisquis ubique habitat, Max-
ime, nusquam habitat.*[200] Montaigne quotes the
line and enlarges upon the predicament of the
man who lives nowhere. Here, too, is Candidus,[201] Maynard's Jean, who *solus habes* this
and *solus habes* that, but *uxorem habes cum
populo.* Candidus appears, under aliases, in
Marot and Opitz, in Owen, Weckherlin, Be-
nassú Montanari and in many another modern
epigrammatist. Not all Martial's boasters are
of the male sex. Fabulla,[202] for instance, is so
fatally conscious of her youth and beauty and
riches, like Coleridge's Anne,

> Sweet Anne! The knowledge of thy wealth
> Reduces thee to poverty.

Weckherlin's Ross, girls of Tscherning, Kongehl, Celander, Mencke, Opitz and Marot are
among the early descendants of Fabulla, and
her line still flourishes.

Crispinus' unique and glorious purple cloak
has been stolen.[203] A dangerous theft, that of
such a garment! *Qua possis melius fallere,
sume togam* — "A safer trick it were to take
a toga," says Martial to the thief, so giving the
Spanish Friar its motto. Charmenion,[204] curled,
depilated, lisping, insists on addressing Martial as "Brother." "Stop it, or I'll call you
'Sister'!" *Bellus* Sabellus, apparently the
original of Boufflers' Beauveau and Deveau,
is treated to a whole series of assonant insults:

> I *loathe you, you are such a beau, Lebeau.*
> D*isgusting things are beaux, and so Lebeau.*
> I'*d rather know war's woe than know Lebeau.*
> Pr*ay decompose, my beau Lebeau, below.*[205]

The word play and assonance of this epigram
on *bellus* Sabellus remind one of Byron's epitaph on John Adams, the careless carrier, who
carried his can to his mouth with such frequency that

> *the liquor he drank, being too much for one,*
> He *could not carry off* — *so he's now carri-on.*

But it is Cotilus [206] who is loveliest of Martial's dandies — Cotilus admits it — Cotilus,

[139]

sleek, perfumed, impeccably clad, humming the latest airs from Egypt and Spain, accomplished in the new dances, acquainted with the racing news, familiar with every scandal, for ever whispering some little secret in a lady's ear —

So this is what makes a man " lovely," you say?
    Of course it seems churlish to doubt it.
But should I choose to pass for a thoroughbred ass,
    I can see how I'd best set about it.

Jonson's Don Surly and many another modern epigrammatic figure are combinations of Cotilus, Cotta,[207] and one or two more of Martial's men about town.

Then come the spendthrifts and voluptuaries. Here is Labienus,[208] Jonson's Groine. Or here is Bassus,[209] later to appear in La Monnoie. Bassus has bought a splendid cloak. " A wonderful bargain! " " Cheap, eh! " " No, charged." Or Saufeius,[210] with all his pomp and circumstance, and his huge train of followers:

May no such train attend you, Marcus!
Feel no pique or gall:
Man needs but little here below;
Besides — they're bailiffs all.

Or, introduced to us by Paschasius and Anselmus, also, Ammianus,[211] whose father had re-
cently died and left his son nothing but a most
suggestive coil of rope, thereby contriving to
bring genuine sorrow to the young prodigal.
And Laetinus [212] whose fever stays with him
day after day, entertained as it is by so much
luxury and pleasure and drink. Laetinus is
rather like Rousseau's drunkard whose doctor
wishes to cure him first of his bibacity, then of
his fever:

> My fever, doctor, is your care;
> As for my thirst, that's my affair.

Philomusus [213] used to be on an allowance but
now inherits a fortune from his father. Tanta-
mount to being disinherited, poor fellow! *Omnia,
Castor, emis: sic fiet ut omnia vendas;* [214] Jonson quotes this epigram as illustrating that
" sometimes one verse alone makes a perfect
poem; " it serves as a motto for the *Connoisseur;* " Who buys without discretion, buys to
sell," writes Dr. Johnson. Acerra [215] smells of
wine. Not of yesterday's wine, though, —
heavens, no! For Acerra, like Lessing's tippler,
like tipplers of Opitz and Kongehl and Weckherlin, always makes a point of drinking till

daybreak. Fescennia [216] is in bad condition, too, but tries to conceal the scent of her potations with pastilles, as do inebriates of Weckherlin, again, and of Sir Thomas More — to approach no nearer to current practice. Have done with futile fraud and be simply drunk! Or Pollio [217] — Pollio has his likeness to William Walsh's Thraso:

Thraso picks quarrels when he's drunk at night;
When sober in the morning, dares not fight.
Thraso, to shun those ills that may ensue,
Drink not at night, or drink at morning too.

Martial's best known coward is Fannius,[218] who ran away from the battlefield so scared that he killed himself. Butler's men, who,

> *when they're out of hopes of flying,*
> *Will run away from death by dying,*

seem similar to Fannius, as well as to Seneca's soldiers, *quidam timore mortis cogantur ad mortem.* Montaigne quotes this epigram, his translator rendering the last line:

Can there be greater madness, pray reply,
Than that one should, for fear of dying, die?

Denham, in his *Of Old Age*, may have had Fannius in mind when he wrote,

Such madness as for fear of death to die,
Is, to be poor for fear of poverty,

as may Francis Quarles in his *Hieroglyphics*
where he comments on the uselessness of a
physician to him who is well:

But to make a trade of trying
  Drugs and doses, always pruning,
Is to die for fear of dying.
  He's untun'd, that's always tuning.

But enough of Fannius — treading on his
hurried heels come a troop of gift and legacy
and dowry hunters. Here is Naevia,[219] coughing
and wheezing, but really not at all consumptive, merely wheedling her hunter. Here is
Polycharmus [220] who gets sick ten times a year
in order to extract presents from friends on his
recoveries. Like Smith's complainant, Martial
cannot " afford to waste so much time on a
mortuary uncertainty." Be decent, Polycharmus: get sick now — just once more. Gargilianus,[221] the Lidio of Frigimelica-Roberti,
sends gifts to rich old bachelors and widows
and desires to be considered philanthropic:

The worm on the hook is a " gift " to the fish,
  And the bait to the bear, then, I take it?

[143]

I*f it still is not clear what a " gift " is, see here —
I am poor, need a present. Now make it!*

Marianus,[222] Lessing's Avar, is advised, if he
wishes to make his " captator " honestly mourn
his death, to leave him nothing. Pontilianus,[223]
like Domenico Cervelli's friend, uses Martial
and promises him a legacy when he's dead.
Martial and Cervelli, though wanting nothing,
positively nothing, really, exclaim in unison,
" Then die! " Maro also is given to understand,
less bluntly, that a funeral is in order:

> A*live, you give me naught,*
> A*t death a legacy.*
> T*he tongue of a fool could utter*
> T*he thoughts that arise in me.*[224]

Maro at least gives a motto to the *Rambler,* as
well as epigrams to Owen, Abel Evans, and a
half dozen German poets of the seventeenth
century. Numa, of whom Thomas Bastard also
tells, goes further than Maro toward obliging
the poet:

W*hen his pyre was constructed, and spices were
    bought
  And his weeping wife fainted and fell,*

When embalmers were there, and his bier *had been*
    brought,
  Numa *made me his heir — and got well.*[225]

Saleianus [226] and Paetus,[227] like an acquaint-
ance of Herrick's, are hardly able to bear up
under the loss of their wives, whose decease has
left them millionaires. Martial is all sympathy.
Dreadful! Dreadful! I am desolated that this
has happened to *you!* Phileros, known to Lessing and other epigrammatists of his time, is
also growing wealthy:

In *the soil of your farm are your seven rich wives,*
  All in urns.
That *farm never yielded to anyone else*
  Such returns.[228]

Even Martial himself professes to be in the
ranks of his dowry hunters, with Lessing, Homburg, Scherffer, Müller, Giucci, and Nícoli-
Cristiani close beside him:

    I *hesitate to marry Paula.*
      Paula seems much bolder.
    She's *too old. I'd marry Paula,*
      Were she only older.[229]

Behind these mercenary rascals comes a
troupe of hypocrites of different ilk. Here is
Caelius,[230] the client, who got tired of early

morning calls and therefore pretended to be suffering from gout. He suffered so realistically that at last he actually did become gouty — one of the first recorded cases of the influence of mind upon body, which Montaigne records again in his *De ne Contrefaire le Malade*. Here is Gaurus,[231] adducing this, that, and the other famous man who was addicted to some one of his own vices. You imbibe too freely. Yes, but so did Cato:

> *Gaurus pretends to Cato's fame*
> *And proves, by Cato's vice, his claim,*

as Dr. Johnson translates the line used as a motto for the *Rambler*. Every other minor vice of Gaurus seems to have had its victims among the great and good. But which of these men you cite was addicted to that major vice of yours, Gaurus, a vice which you do not mention, and which really is unmentionable? Coleridge's epigram fits Gaurus:

Tho' few like Fox can speak — like Pitt can think —
Yet all like Fox can game — like Pitt can drink.

Pannychus [232] and Chrestos,[233] like Francis Thynne's *Puritane*, prate loudly of idealistic philosophy and the austere life, and confine

their virtue to their public utterances. Pannychus may not depilate his body, but his mind
is depilated.[234] Aper,[235] Herrick's " thrifty Mr.
Prig," thought liquor an abomination, when he
was poor; now that he is rich, he seldom man-
ages to get home, even of an afternoon, without being half-seas over. Gellia,[236] who appears
in Wernicke and Opitz too, has no tears for her
father's death in private; but in company, oh
dear me! " He grieves most truly that does
grieve alone," as Fletcher renders Martial's
conclusion.

Then there follows a long train of reprobates
who fall barely short of being out and out
criminals. Linus, for instance, of whom Rabutin also tells us:

Just GIVE *Linus half what he asks as a loan,*
Then console
Yourself with the thought you had better lose half
Than the whole.[237]

Martial's crew of infamous rascals with un-
savory habits is large. Many of them shipped
again with modern epigrammatists, but as in
the case of a Teniers village scene, it is best not
to scrutinize them too closely.

His actual criminals, however, are quite pre-

sentable. There is Tongilianus [238] whose house
burned down. Donations from sympathetic
friends bring him five times the sum it cost.
Who could have set the fire? Fuller cites Tongilianus' case in connection with the tinners of
Cornwall. There is Vacerra,[239] Herrick's Bore-
man, an informer, blackmailer, perjurer, pimp,
profligate, master of gladiators — and still not
rich! Or Zoilus once more, as Addison Angli-
cizes him:

Thy beard and head are of a different dye;
Short of one foot, distorted in an eye;
With all these tokens of a knave complete,
Should'st thou be honest, thou'rt a dev'lish cheat.[240]

And here is Cilix [241] the thief, so industrious,
so filled with professional pride, that, rather
than return empty-handed, he carries off a
large statue of Priapus — a theft equivalent to
that of stealing a policeman. On and on they
file, murderers such as Chrestilla and Fabius
bringing up the rear:

Chrestilla has buried her husbands,
  While Fabius has buried his wives.
Since they both always make every wedding a
    wake,
  Pray, Venus, unite their two lives.[242]

But worse than respectable, hard-working criminals are stingy plutocrats. There are the friends [243] who take offence at you, finding it cheaper than making you presents. There is Cinna [244] who neither grants you a loan nor quickly refuses one, and Sextus [245] who precludes one, even a request for one, by muttering an audible soliloquy about his debts and poverty. Or here is Diodorus,[246] Nícoli-Cristiani's Mevio, who had gout in the feet; on getting into a lawsuit, he failed to pay his lawyer. Must be gout in the hands, remarks Martial, followed by Owen and Marot and Herrick. Postumus [247] is not always stingy, but rich gifts wax poor when givers prove remindful. He is Prior's John:

> To *John I* ow'd *great obligation*,
>   But *John unhappily thought* fit
> To *publish it to all the nation:*
>   Sure *John and I are more than quit.*

And there is Candidus,[248] ready, so he swears, to share any adversity with a friend, but meanwhile keeping a firm and solitary grip upon his own prosperity. And Gellius, [249] who is forever putting a new screw or nail in his house, so that he may repel borrowers with that immortal excuse, " I am building." And Scaevola,[250] who, like Coleridge's friend, " his mirth all gone, his kindness, his discretion," comes into an estate only to be not its possessor but possession, and despite his previous vows to heaven that, once rich, he would be a mighty philanthropist, acts as if he had lost rather than gained a fortune. " Either live, thief, or pay the Gods back."

Stingy hosts, in particular, are anathema. Calenus,[251] poor, used to give his friends good meals; rich, by the inheritance of a million, his meals are awful. His friends pray that he may now inherit a few more millions: then he will die of starvation. Auctus [252] is by way of being an antiquary, not one like Donne's,

If in his studie he hath so much care
To hang old strange things, let his wife beware,

but one who collects old strange silver, upon the history of which he lingers until his guests grow parched:

" With this beaker at Carthage Aeneas was pledged
By his hostess, the beautiful Dido."
When he gets you enthused, then from jars
Priam used
He pours you a drink fit for — Fido.

There are hosts such as Annius [253] who has scudding servants that skip by you so fast that you cannot help yourself to the food you fancy, and you get only peripatetic meals like Pope's dinner at Timon's villa, "in plenty starving, tantalized in state." There are other hosts who serve you quite a different bill of fare than that which they themselves enjoy:

You employ yourself gayly with turbot, while I
Am expected to relish a sprat:
A crow from its cage, where it died of old age,
Comes to me; you have squabs browned and fat.[254]

Other hosts, still, serve you nothing at all: they are like Pope's Old Cotta, "whose kitchen vied in coolness with his grot." Here is one canny soul who has a noble house and grounds — but no dining or sleeping rooms. *Quam bene non habitas!* [255] Jonson contrasts such inhospitable estates with *Penshurst:*

Those proud ambitious heaps, and nothing else,
May say, their lords have built, but thy lord dwells.

Blenheim House, according to Pope, or Abel Evans, was one such "proud ambitious heap,"

> Thanks, sir, cried I, 'tis very fine,
> But where d'ye sleep, or where d'ye dine?
> I find by all you have been telling
> That 'tis a house, but not a dwelling,

and Lord Hervey makes Cheswick another. Martial complains to one such host, who shelters his plants in lovely greenhouses, protects his very trees with glass, yet treats the poet rather less humanely:

> In a cell I am bunked,
> With one window — defunct;
> If he slept there, old Boreas would sneeze.
> If this is the best you will do for your guest,
> Why, the next time I'll visit your trees.[256]

Even more irritating is Ligurinus [257] whose guests must listen to his verse throughout the meal. Like Prior with his Topaz (Sir Richard Blackmore), Martial could say: " Full hardly earneth Mart his dinner."

Martial knew all about poverty. Rather ruefully he remarks to Aemilianus upon the general situation, and rather ruefully does Dr. Johnson translate the remark:

> Once poor, my friend, still poor you must remain,
> The rich alone have all the means of gain.[258]

The makeshifts and subterfuges, the outward awkwardnesses and inward emotions of poor men were perfectly familiar to him. He would have enjoyed Caleb Balderstone. There is Cotta,[259] Herrick's "warie Mr. Rush," who proclaimed that his shoes had twice been stolen, at the baths, from the one careless slave who is his household:

He, *being a man very sharp and astute —*
  Just the words that he used, do not doubt
    them —
Devised a shrewd scheme for retaining his shoes:
He now comes to dinner without them.

Poor Cinna,[260] La Martinière's Codrus, takes such slim meals that Martial affects to believe that, just as Mithridates used to take doses of poison to immune himself from death by poison, so Cinna takes ever so small doses of food to immune himself from death by starvation. Cinna appears again [261] in a one-line epigram which Addison, treating of *Nonsense,* uses to illustrate his point; which Jonson quotes as again exemplifying the perfect one-line poem; which Dryden alludes to in his *Essay of Dramatic Poesy;* which even Colley Cibber translates, and better, Lovelace:

[153]

> *Cinna seems poor in show,*
> *And he is so.*

Gargilianus has simply nothing, no this, no that:

> *Whence the cash for your taking your girl on a*
> *lark?*
> *For your rent for that hole in the wall?*
> *" I live in a well-reasoned way," you remark.*
> *What's your reason for living at all?* [262]

It reminds one of Piron's indifference to the indifferent poet who, urged to desist from writing, replies that he must live. " We do not see the necessity of it."

Among the poorest of the poor, usually, are the parasites, the professional diners-out. Martial, as a client, had plenty of opportunity to note their failures and successes. Aper,[263] for instance, buys a shack which an owl would hate to inhabit, but it is near Maro's villa, so Aper hopes, if not for life, at least for dinner. Selius [264] prowls around woebegone as if he had lost all he owned, including his wife and children: he has not yet located a host for the evening meal. Menogenes [265] does menial service at the athletic field for his intended host, extols his defects, calls his towels, though

[154]

"dirtier than a baby's bib," whiter than driven snow, to get at last a weary, "Well, come along." Oh, these friends of yours, friends of your boar, your mullet, your sow's udder, your oysters — friends of whom Logau and Sutor and Martini also tell! "Dined I so well, they would be friends of mine." [266] The best known of them, perhaps, is Philomusus, [267] Jonson's Mime and Captain Hungry, who is invited everywhere as an entertainer: "Men love thee not for this; they laugh at thee." One of Philomusus' services is that of newsmonger. [268] He is the original of Davies' Smell-feast Afer,

No sooner is a ship at sea surpris'd
But straight he learns the news and doth disclose
*   it;*
No sooner hath the Turk devis'd
To conquer Christendom, but straight he knows it,

and bears some resemblance to Prior's Chameleon, whose

wisdom sets all Europe right,
And teaches Marlborough when to fight.

Physical peculiarities, as well as peculiarities of disposition and circumstance, have always provided good copy for wits. Thersites prob-

[155]

ably was aware of this fact, as were Pericles and Julius Caesar. Martial's freaks are no small part of his "biggest show on earth." Poor Matrinia [269] wants to know if the poet can't be fond of oldish women. "Why, yes. But you are not an antique, Matrinia; you are remains." Afra,[270] like Baldi's aging damsel, gaily calls everyone "Mama" or "Daddy," though really old enough to be the great-grand-mama of all of them. Lesbia's years are also a matter of infinite calculation:

> *You were born when gruff Brutus was consul?*
> *Excuse me, dear madam, you lie.*
> *Oh! Born in the reign of king Numa?*
> *Once more now! King Numa? Fie, fie!*
> *Come, Lesbia, come now, be candid;*
> *You clearly are not such a bud;*
> *If looks are to be my informants,*
> *You were made of Promethean mud.*[271]

The exaggeration reminds one of Chapelle's epigram on Ninon de L'Enclos: "No wonder she can discourse upon the philosophy of Plato so intimately: she very likely lived with him."

Then there are the victims of bad breath or of other personal odours, excusable or inexcusable. Postumus, Lessing's Herr von Dampf, patronizingly saunters up:

"My *lips, or hand, kiss which you choose* —
  It does not matter."
It does not. Either way I lose.
I'll try the latter.[272]

It is Manneia,[273] perhaps — then we may leave these unfragrant unfortunates — who receives the worst treatment of any of Martial's ladies. Yet Marot and Weckherlin and Lessing are among the later writers who have had no scruples in ascribing Manneia's misfortune to modern ladies. Coleridge's imitation is gentle:

Thy lap-dog, Rufa, is a dainty beast,
It don't surprise me in the least
To see thee lick so dainty clean a beast.
But that so dainty clean a beast licks thee,
Yes — this surprises me.

La Martinière's Aurèle, who was bitten by a serpent, to the regret of the reptile, and Goldsmith's man who was bitten by a mad dog —

  The man recovered from the bite,
  The dog it was that died —

seem to be blood relatives of Manneia.

Then there are the people lacking the regular complement of natural teeth. Maximina [274] is amongst them. Ovid's advice, " Smile, maiden, smile, an thou wouldst be wise," is not meant for you, even if you were still a maiden, Maximina: you simply *must* not show those gums; no comedies, no jokes, no parties for you; attend tragedies, visit the afflicted, go to funerals; "Weep, maiden, weep, an *thou* wouldst be wise." Lessing tells of Maximina, too, and her youthful arts seem to have been helpful to Jonson in *Sejanus*. Suggestive of Major Pendennis, or of Tony Bagstock, is Martial's old beau,[275] timeworn and artificial, who reclines on the couch yonder, jauntily employing a toothpick. It's a bluff: " he hasn't a single tooth there." Aelia now is equally destitute:

Two of your teeth were blown out by a cough,
  And a subsequent cough blew out two.
You can now cough away, Aelia, all night and day:
  There is nothing a third cough can do.[276]

Or, as Richard Crashaw translates the last two lines:

This last cough, Aelia, coughed out all thy fear,
Thou'st left a third cough now no business here.

[158]

Owen, Marot and Harington, Opitz, Weckherlin and Herrick are among the other modern
poets who have refused to let the poor lady rest
in peace.

Next come those familiar persons who can't
do a thing with their hair. Labienus, you look
like a three-headed monstrosity,

*With that great shock of hair over each of your
 ears —
 By it even a girl would be graced! —
And your top destitute of the tiniest shoot,
 A perfectly pastureless waste.*[277]

You may be able to get away with three por-
tions of food at a dinner party, but mind you
don't get near the Arcade of Philippus, or the
statue of Hercules will see you, take you for
Geryon, and bring you to an untimely end.
Phoebus[278] anoints his bald head with a thick
ointment, but " it's clear that a sponge is his
barber." Laetinus,[279] of whom Addison and
Jeremy Taylor also tell, dyes his whitening
locks, but Proserpine " will strip thy hoary
noddle of its mask." Fabulla[280] swears her
curls are her own. They are. She paid for them,
like Prior's Pontia and like many another mod-

ern lady, including some in the museums of Weckherlin and Harington and Brébeuf.

Close to Fabulla are the painted, and otherwise refurbished, ladies — Vetustilla,[281] whose bodily blemishes, minutely chronicled, are so numerous and irremediable that she really should assume that she has adequate grounds for ending her long quest of a husband; Galla,[282] who, at night, puts herself away in boxes, who does not sleep with her own face. They remind one of Swift's *Beautiful Young Nymph Going to Bed,* of the denizen of his *Lady's Dressing Room,* of his *Progress of Beauty,* and of those heroines of Brébeuf, one of whom starts on a journey carelessly forgetting to take along her gloves, teeth, and visage.

But enough of these uncomely creatures, and enough of Martial's butts in general. Few types of person, few human traits, few vocations that ever have been ridiculed escaped that Roman wit. Here is that innkeeper at dry Ravenna whom Addison and Dr. Warton quote:

> *There's a shrewd old fox at Ravenna,*
> *Who cheated me of late.*
> *When I asked for claret and water,*
> *He gave me claret straight.*[283]

There is that barber whose slowness gave
Voiture a chance to twit Vaugelas on his belated translation of Quintus Curtius — *altera
barba subit:*

By the time the barber Eurus
  Had circled Lupo's face,
    A second beard had sprouted
      In the first one's place.[284]

Architects and artists, jugglers and jockeys,
acrobats and auctioneers, cobblers, hawkers,
beggars, moneylenders, shoppers!

  So with the rest. Who will may trace
  Behind the new each elder face
        Defined as clearly;
  Science proceeds, and man stands still;
  Our " world " to-day's as good or ill, —
        As vulgar (nearly)
  As yours was, Martial! You alone,
  Who knew us all, we have not known.[285]

V. THE ANTIQUITY OF MODERN WIT

FEW things are more sobering than to read through a collection of jokes at one sitting. Martial, it may be interjected, was very conscious of this fact: though each of his books shows great variety of theme and treatment, though he constantly turns from grave to gay, from lively to severe, he nevertheless pleads, and pleads again, to be read at just the time and for just the time that best suits his readers. But if there is anything more tristful than the long-continued perusal of funny stories, it is likely to be some laborious explanation of why a thing seems funny, anyhow. By the time we are fully instructed in the fine and dubious distinctions between the comic, humorous, witty, and satiric, we may be disposed to doubt the veritable existence of any emotion save melancholy. Once we have learned precisely how to classify and file away a laugh, we are apt to wonder who on earth wants to laugh.

Seriously, very seriously, while there luckily is a demand somewhere for books entitled, *Physiologie und Psychologie des Lachens und des Komischen,* or *Le rire; essai sur la signification du comique,* that demand does not usually come from professional humorists or from those who wish to be amused. We may admire Emerson, but his theories on *The Comic,* whatever else they do, do not increase our satisfaction in a joke; even Meredith's *Essay on Comedy and the Uses of the Comic Spirit* hardly adds to our enjoyment of even *The Egoist;* and as for a book like Freud's *Der Witz und Seine Beziehung zum Unbewussten* — it may, perhaps, be left to the scholar with safety, but not to the average citizen who wishes to preserve his own reason for laughing, or his reason at all. But if a Leigh Hunt or a Mark Twain or a Lowell, Butler, Thackeray, or Lamb wishes to tell us, simply and deliciously, some of the more immediate causes of laughter, we can listen without peril. Even if an Aristotle or a Kant, wishing to give us its one fundamental, comprehensive cause, tells us that the ludicrous always is an unexpected contrast between perfection and imperfection, completeness and incompleteness, in a matter

[163]

insufficiently serious to occasion serious emotion, we may hear them, pensively, perhaps, but quite unspoiled.

It is not our present design, fortunately, to emulate any such men — not even Lamb or Aristotle! — but merely to show that whatever be the distinction between wit and humour, whatever be the underlying psychology of it all, Martial was acquainted with almost every general method of extracting a smile or a laugh that is employed by modern writers. Even this is a project sufficiently ambitious, perhaps, and one that is apt to be more than sufficiently tedious.

Martial was primarily a wit, rather than a humorist, and much of his, as of any man's, wit is not at all funny, or intended to be funny. Its reward is an intellectual appreciation, not an emotional reaction. With this sort of wit, which may even be reflective and serious, we are not now concerned, but only with the wit that is meant to amuse. Now we are amused, of course, both by what one says and by his way of saying it. Some stories, to be sure, seem so funny in themselves that they simply cannot be quite ruined in the telling, unless the lady happens to forget the point entirely. Conversely, some mode of expression, some happy phrase, some absurd word play, like Porson's invited impromptu on the Latin gerund —

When Dido found Aeneas would not come,
She mourned in silence and was Di-do-dum —

may seem so amusing in themselves as to make us feel that nothing more is needed. But generally speaking, both the form and the content are rather inseparable sources of amusement. Also nearly inseparable from anything that amuses us is some degree or species of incongruity, of surprise, of point. Here again the part may often seem to be almost the whole. " I proposed to that girl and would have married her, if it hadn't been for something she said." " What did she say? " " No."

Philaenis weeps with just one eye.
Queer, is it not?
You wish you knew the reason why?
That's all she's got.[286]

" Afraid you are going to have insomnia? What are the symptoms? " " Twins." " Claudia would be quite as tall as Nero's colossal statue, if she were only eighteen inches — shorter." [287]

The vineyards are fruitful in parts of the land,
  Thanks to the showers that came.
The vintner Coranus has bottled a lot
  Of — the same.[288]

But aware as we are of these general attributes of wit and humour, aware that the same subject may be treated in a large variety of amusing ways, sardonically, sympathetically, whimsically, and also aware that the same joke may have made laughable elements and aspects — facts which make either a very zealous, or a very casual, attempt to classify jokes an undertaking itself rather humorous — let us try to see somewhat specifically how our wits and humorists do amuse us, what their subjects are, what methods they use to bring out the ludicrous possibilities in those subjects.

We find that one of their most fertile themes is what may briefly, if broadly, be called misfortunes, misfortunes usually so trifling as not to summon tears. Yet even tragedy and near-tragedy also, we know, may often be made to seem comic, in print as in cartoons. The Irishman, during his fall from the top of the ten-story building, is certainly on his way to being a dead Hibernian, but we smile at his hopeful comment as he passes the fourth floor, "All roight, so far!" A funeral is imminent when Picentinus, the Bluebeard, marries the almost equally dexterous Galla —

Of the husbands that Galla has laid in the grave
    A conservative number is seven,
But her marriage to you proves it touchingly true
    That she wishes to join them in heaven — [289]

but neither we nor Martial take the situation seriously. Much printed humour, we observe, especially that dealing with some physical calamity like this Irishman's, is almost visual. *"The belated traveller* (surprised by a bull as he takes a short cut to the station): By Jove! I believe I shall catch that train after all!" We can *see* that man, with his earnest but mixed emotions, as he tears across that field.

The bathkeeper Dasius keeps tabs on his trade:
He charged chubby Spatale triple. She paid.[290]

We can *see* poor Spatale, flushed, angry, outraged, but above all things eager to escape further attention, fumbling for those extra coins.

These ludicrous misfortunes are of every kind and degree — all sorts of embarrassing predicaments, of unlucky ventures, of personal oddities, suggested, betrayed, described, caricatured, all sorts of human weaknesses, parsimony, vanity, self-righteousness, shyness, selfishness, priggishness, prudery, insincerity, carelessness, curiosity, ineptitude. Here is the sudden discomfiture of the modern gentleman in the barber's chair who has commented favorably upon the affection that makes the barber's dog stay so near his master. "It ain't that, Sir, but sometimes I makes a mistake and nicks a piece of a customer's ear off, and he likes to be handy." Or there is the irritating contretemps of that ancient personage splendidly attired yet strangely intercepted when he was sauntering into the aristocrats' section of the theatre:

Just as gorgeous Euclides indignant exclaimed
  That his lands brought him thousands a year,
That his ancestors all were men wealthy and famed
  Whose descent from fair Leda was clear;
As he thus showed the usher a seat was his right
  As the pride of the Roman élite,
There fell from the pouch of this rich noble knight
  A — permit to vend in the street.[291]

One of the most common of these misfortunes at which we laugh is ignorance. Our amusing grammatical atrocities, lingual catastrophes and dialectal abortions are hardly more than foreshadowed in Martial, or in other ancient writers. It is chiefly the modern Anglo-Saxon, in fact, who finds comedy in the tragic mutilation of his native tongue. But ignorance revealed in almost every other way, misunderstandings, mistakes, dullness, irrationality, is very frequently a source of amusement for Martial, though less frequently than for our own wits. A favorite form of irrationality is some ridiculous choice of means to gain an end. The sea-sick passenger asks the steward to present his compliments to the chief engineer and inquire if there is any hope of the boilers blowing up. The distressed mother tells her little boy, shrieking in the dentist's chair, that he must behave at once, or she'll never, never take him to the dentist's again.

> TORQUATUS, *four miles from the city,*
>   *Owns a country seat costly and grand:*
> *Four miles from the city, Otillus*
>   *Bought a cot and an acre of land.*

> *Torquatus built baths of rich marble,*
>   *So large as to do for a club:*
> *Otillus installed then, undaunted,*
>   *A superfine second-hand tub.*

[169]

Torquatus had laurel groves planted;
Each tree was well-leaved and full grown:
As soon as he saw them, Otillus
Had a hundred of horse chestnuts sown.

Torquatus was next chosen consul:
Otillus was boss of his ward,
And inwardly felt more than certain
That now poor Torquatus was floored.

I fear it will end like the fable
Where the frog with ambition was curst
To rival the ox in dimensions:
There is danger Otillus will burst.[292]

The irrational explanation or solution, the silly question, the naïve remark, the absurd excuse, the illogical argument, stupidity of every sort — no doubt a sense of our own superiority contributes to our delight in it. The gentleman who is incensed at the bank's discourtesy and threatens to withdraw his — his — his — overdraft and the tramp who requests " 'elp for a poor man whose wife is out o' work " are amusingly " ignorant " in much the same way that Martial is amusingly " ignorant " when, reproached for having lost his client's case because he made such a mess of it, he demands a still higher fee because he made such an ass of himself [293] in the process, or when he establishes the etiquette to be followed with Myrtale who vainly tries to conceal her potations by chewing laurel leaves:

So now when you meet her with rubicund face
    And with eyes that can look but not see,
And with veins large and dark, it's correct to re-
    mark:
    " Ah, Myrt! Drunk again? On a tree! " [294]

The instructor in the business college tells the new class of the merits of shorthand: " It is a matter of record that it took the poet Gray seven years to write his famous poem, Elegy in a Rural Cemetery. Had he been proficient in stenography, he could have done it in seven minutes. We have had students who have written it in that length of time." The father returns home from his celebration of another prospective domestic event, just as the clock strikes three, to find his anticipations more than gratified. There were triplets. " Oi'm not superstitious," he remarks, " but thank hivin Oi didn't come home at twelve! " The science of numbers is also invoked by Martial:

[171]

Hylas *offered three-fourths when his eyes became*
sore;
Now one's gone, he'll pay half what you lent.
Golden moments soon fly, Quintus; so may that
eye.
If it does, he won't pay you a cent.[295]

" Ya'as, there didn't ought to be no poor," asserts the Hyde Park orator. " We all ought to
be wealthy an' the wealthy starvin' like us."
" Why, Paetus! The idea of me, Martial, being
dunned for that hundred pounds you lent me,
just because you can't collect the two thousand
pounds you lent Bucco! I to suffer for another
fellow's rascality? Not a bit of it! Besides,
your survival of the loss of the two thousand
makes it perfectly clear that you can easily
stand the loss of a hundred more." [296] " I see,
Phoebus, that you have sent me back that
I. O. U. of mine for four thousand pounds.
Thanks awfully, old fellow! But would you
mind making it a cash loan of one thousand
instead? You see, what I owe and can't pay is
my own already." [297] The humane jailer of
whom Horace Walpole tells is less consciously
naïve. Says he to his prisoner: " My good
friend, I have a little favour to ask of you,
which, from your obliging disposition, I doubt

not you will grant. You were ordered for execution a week from Friday. I have a particular engagement on that day, and if it makes no difference to you, would you say next Friday instead? " It is more often assumed than real irrationality that Martial gives us, and to that vast array of modern jokes based on the naïveté of children there is almost no parallel in his pages.

One of the most ludicrous exhibitions of ignorance, real or assumed, is the unfortunate remark which defeats some purpose, betrays some weakness, or reveals some secret of the speaker. Entertaining in much the same way are the irate wife who hisses " Coward! " when her husband takes refuge from her in a lion's cage, and Martial's auctioneer who is suddenly asked why Marcus is selling the farm, anyway:

" *What occasions the sale? Er . . . you see . . . it's like this . . .*
Well, he . . . lost all his crops there . . . slaves . . . sheep . . .
That's the reason, you know, that he hates the place so."
They knew. Marcus still will sell — cheap.[298]

A perfectly tremendous proportion of the stories that amuse us have as their subject misfortunes such as these. And a very large percentage of the remainder is based on a closely related and overlapping theme, on the ridicule of such misfortunes, on what, for brevity's sake, may be termed the insult. Now insults may come in various forms, as Cyrano knew. There is the rather direct sort like that employed by the two urchins: " Huh! Yer mother takes in washin'! " "Well, yer didn't s'pose she'd leave it hangin' aht overnight unless your farver was in prison, did yer? " Martial, too, could be rather direct:

> If by each hair each year were told,
> Old Lydia's a three year old.[299]

Then there is the naïve, or apparently naïve, and unintentional variety, like that in the dog dealer's answer to Mrs. Profiteer's inquiry if that is a pedigree dog: " Pedigree dog? Lor' bless ye, mum, I should think 'e is! Why if that animal could only talk, 'e wouldn't speak to either of us." Martial was familiar with this species also. Oppianus [299a] has begun to write poetry — it must be because he has the poetic pallor. Apparently no other reason for his writing occurs to Martial.

[174]

Though you serve richest wines,
Paulus, rumour opines,
   That they buried your four wives, I think.
It's of course all a lie,
Which I hereby deny.
   No, I really don't care for a drink.[299b]

Often it is some affectation of geniality and
kindliness that carries the insult. Swift tells his
congregation: " My brethren, there are three
sorts of pride — of birth, of riches, and of
talent. I shall not now speak of the latter, none
of you being liable to that abominable vice."
Isabella Wardle is solicitous for the health of
her beloved aunt, who is observed in her en-
deavours to captivate the impressionable Tup-
man: " Have a silk handkerchief, to tie around
your dear old head — you really should take
care of yourself — consider your age."

Philaenis wears dresses of purple all day,
   And she sleeps in a purple gown, too;
But pride she has none, no love of display:
   It's the odour she loves, not the hue.[300]

Insulting innuendo, of course, we find everywhere. The tragedian who is under contract to
tour South Africa mentions the fact to a friend.
" The ostrich," comments the friend reflec-

tively, "lays an egg weighing anywhere from two to four pounds."

> *"Those bandits wronged me," Saenia said.*
> *Each bandit scanned her, shook his head.*[301]

One common weapon in the arsenal of insult, urbane irony, is frequently found, to be sure, in the pages of *Punch*. But urbane irony is one of Martial's best used weapons, also. The rhetorician Apollodotus [302] used to confuse Quintus and Decimus, Crassus and Macer, but now, now — ah, the power of toil and care! — he has thoroughly compiled the four names and learned them. Bumptious Postumus is told:

> *When you kiss me you use only half of your mouth.*
> *I approve. Half that half, though, will do.*
> *Will you grant me a greater, ineffable boon?*
> *Keep the rest of that latter half, too.*[303]

Hazlitt thought Pope's lines on the Lord Mayor's show to be the finest piece of wit of which he knew:

> *Now night descending, the proud scene is o'er,*
> *But lives in Settle's numbers one day more.*

In almost exactly the same ironic tone are Martial's lines on an ancient lady:

Philaenis, thou hadst lived but Nestor's years
   When all untimely thou wert swept below.
The Sibyl's span was not for thee, dear child:
   She was thy elder by three months or so.[304]

There seems to be no mode of insult which the Latin poet overlooked, no shade of insult which he thought unbecoming, from unmitigated barbarity to jovial banter such as that to which he treats Munna, for example, who has a habit of sending, from abroad, casks of atrocious wine to his Roman cronies:

He could buy the best Massic or Setian for less.
   This poison's not cheap as you'd think.
Munna never comes home
   To his friends here at Rome.
He's afraid we would give him a drink.[305]

If it be true that he is over fond of a really ill-tempered jest, it can at least be said in his defence that his victims generally deserved no special clemency. They were usually the sort of persons that Juvenal satirized with still less mercy. Satire, of course, may or may not be amusing, but Martial's moral purpose and righteous indignation, unlike Juvenal's, were seldom so great as to make his satire solemn. Nor was his temperament such as often to let him use satire in the gentle, whimsical fashion of a Charles Lamb. Typical of his amply penetrating tone and manner is one of his epigrams on Zoilus, the rich parvenu, once a runaway slave:

> To *thee, O Saturn, consecrate,*
>   *Jewelled Zoilus gives with praise*
> These *shackles grim, these handcuffs twain —*
>   His *rings of other days.*[306]

If all the wit and humour of the world were collected and analyzed, by some candidate for an asylum, it probably would be found that more than half of it was based on what we have called misfortunes and insults. When one adds that such an analysis would further reveal a large part of the remainder to be based upon what we may call improprieties, certain of our stern forefathers could, it might seem, be forgiven for deeming it rather sinful to smile. Improprieties, however, is a blanket term here used to cover a multitude of sins, not all of them heinous, from the rude, or unfeeling, or cynical remark to the coarsest of sex jokes. Incongruity and surprise play strange tricks upon decorum. Most of us know, to our chagrin, how perversely, and pervertedly, we may

[178]

be seized by a treacherous inclination to laugh at times and things which above most times and things should find us sober! Even a gruesome thing may in some fashion amuse us. The fisherman's wife is told that her husband's body has been found, but found alive with eels. "With eels? Poor dear John! Well, set him again."

How capricious were Nature and Art to poor Nell!
She was painting her cheeks at the time her nose
*   fell.*

His reputation being, with his enemies, what it unfortunately, and, on the whole, unjustly is, we may take it for granted that Martial knew, quite as well as modern wits, the entire range of humorous possibilities that rest in improprieties, from shifty device and clever lie to what should be, by every canon of morals and of taste, simply revolting. One may illustrate the first by such an epigram as that on the medical practitioner, Herodes:

> *The doctor stole his patient's flask.*
> *   When caught, he cried unblinking:*
> *"You reckless fool! Explain at once!*
> *   How dared you dream of drinking?"* [307]

One may not illustrate the last. Whether through piety or oversight, however, Martial's improprieties rarely include the sacrilegious joke which is now so common. Nasidianus,[308] to be sure, whose dire dreams about Martial are bankrupting him through purificatory charges, is told either to stay awake or else dream about himself; and it is with no marked reverence that the poet addresses a caveat to Priapus whose statue — in this case of wood — was supposed to protect an estate from pilferers:

No *vineyard or garden hast thou in thy care,*
  But a grove is watched over by thee.
Priapus, remember that thou wert born there —
  And another Priapus may be.
Priapus, protect this rare grove of thy race,
  Guard it well from hands itching for pelf,
Preserve all its trees for its owner's fireplace —
  If you don't, well, you're wooden yourself.[309]

Misfortunes, insults, improprieties. At first glance, it seems an unlikely as well as an un-Christian trilogy to elicit the bulk of a whole world's laughter. Yet if what we may term drolleries be added to make the trilogy a tetralogy, the subjects of a whole world's wits and humorists do appear to be very nearly accounted for. The chief remaining source of our amusement is the great one which contributes so vastly to our enjoyment of this tetralogy of constantly coalescing subjects, the source which we may — again sacrificing precision to convenience — call phrasing. Now while there are plenty of droll ideas at large which seem to be droll in themselves, almost apart from the mode in which they are expressed, it appears to be generally true that whimsicality, grotesquerie, drollery, is less a subject than a tone, more a humorous manner than humorous material, and is therefore even more closely connected with phrasing than are the other members of the tetralogy. At any rate, deeming it desirable to avoid a discussion such as developed in that celebrated and protracted debate between Holland and Zeeland upon the question, "Does the cod take the hook, or does the hook take the cod?" we intend, without further explanation or apology, to consider drolleries in conjunction with phrasing.

Among the oldest, the most enduring, and the most endured, kinds, or vehicles, of wit is word play in its different forms, down to the lowly pun. Lord Erskine's gallant couplet to Lady Payne at whose house he was taken sick,

'Tis true I am ill, but I need not complain,
For he never knew pleasure who never knew Payne,

Lowell's comment on the schoolmaster " who regarded the birch as a kind of usher to the laurel," Peter Pindar's rejoinder to the doctor who prescribed asses' milk for him,

It cured yourself — I grant it true;
But then — 'twas mother's milk to you,

are only a few well-known examples of a kind of wit familiar to the ancient world, to the present world, and indubitably to a world to come. Martial, naturally, contributes his quota, amongst them his dig at Quintus,

You were legally bound to buy Laelia off,
Or to make her your partner for life.
You perforce took a spouse, so you have in your
house
A really legitimate wife,[310]

or at Rufus, the stingy host,

Rufus said the hare was rare,
And bade them bring his whip.

> It *cost him more to cut his hare*
> *Than give his cook a clip.*[311]

Verbal quirks of every kind one finds in the epigrams.

> A*per pierced his wife's heart with an arrow —*
> *While fooling, they rule.*
> T*he wife, as it happened, was wealthy.*
> *He knows how to fool.*[312]

Even Heine's notorious *double entendre* in acknowledgment of the receipt of a book from its author — " I shall lose no time in reading it " — has its parallel in more than one of Martial's remarks under similar circumstances. He tells Septicianus:

> Y*ou return me my book all unrolled to the end.*
> *You have read it! 'Tis palpably shown!*
> I *know it, believe it, rejoice, and commend.*
> *I have likewise read five of your own.*[313]

A common kind of verbal play is to give some unexpected interpretation, application, twist, to another's words. " Did he leave her much? " the widow's friend was asked. " Nearly every night." " The next person who interrupts the proceedings will be expelled from the court room," announced the judge.

" Hooray! " yelled the prisoner. " I must be inoculated with dullness today," petulantly exclaimed Sergeant K., having made two or three mistakes while conducting a case. " Inoculated, brother! " said Erskine. " I thought you had it in the natural way."

> You always say " It's nothing" when
> For favours you apply.
> If sure it's nothing that you ask,
> Then nothing I'll deny,[314]

says Martial to Cinna. " I called you an unnatural lecher, Coracinus? I? Good heavens, no! I never did! I'll take oath I didn't! I should never dream of such a thing! All I did was to call you a — (and Martial uses a much worse epithet)." [315] " Philo is so awfully popular! He swears he never, never dines at home. And it's true. He never, never dines at all, unless he's asked out." [316]

> So you think to lend me money,
> When you have it by the sack,
> Is a proof of noble friendship?
> Yes, in me, to pay it back.[317]

La Rochefoucauld informs us that " old men like to give good advice as a consolation for no longer being in condition to give a bad example." Antithesis of course is a form of phrasing which may embellish jests on almost any theme. Epigrammatic verse almost inevitably abounds in antithesis, and that of Martial's is no exception. Gellia, for instance, is warned not to assume that *she's* her rare perfume: " it smells the same when sprinkled on my hound." [318] An insistent poet is told:

You read us your verse with your throat wrapped
    in wool.
  The reason we're anxious to know.
    To us it appears
    That some wool in our ears
Would really be more apropos.[319]

It is said that Sheridan, on one occasion when he left his club at night and was proceeding unsteadily homeward, noticed a policeman eyeing him. He lurched toward the officer and gravely entrusted him with a confidence: " My name is Wilberforce. I am a religious man. Don't expose me." Cosconius [320] complains of the excessive length of Martial's epigrams. " Nothing," replies Martial, " is too long from which nothing can be taken away. Now you yourself, my dear fellow, manage to make a distich long." Postumus always is redolent of myrrh, but Martial doubts whether " men who always smell well can smell well." [321] Maronilla, rich and homely, has one comprehensive virtue in Gemellus' eyes — her consumptive cough.[322]

> " Fool for Sale," read the placard.
> The price was immense.
> But I bought him. Repay me.
> Your fool has got sense.[323]

Hood's old Sailor's " head was turned and so he chewed his pigtail till he died; " Prior's inebriate awakes in the fatal skiff, thinks it all a mistake, and wants to be ferried back:

> " Trim the boat and sit quiet," stern Charon replied:
> " You may have forgot, you were drunk when you died; "

one of Martial's thieves is described as being so industrious that, failing better game, he circumvents his own slave and steals his own shoes.[324]

Paradoxical " drolleries," such as these, it seems hardly fitting to include under " phrasing." The same admission must be made regarding certain other amiable inanities which are rather more of a staple with modern humorists than with Martial, though he too can be cheerfully inane. " That pair are so monstrous ugly that if they married, I am sure they would scare each other half to death." [325] " If I'm called a cruel glutton for beating a cook just for serving me a bad meal, what on earth am I to beat a cook for, anyhow? " [326] " Sextilianus would consume all the water there is, if it were not for the fact that he always drinks his wine neat." [327] " Lygdus, I hope you'll — you'll — you'll carry the sunshade of a one-eyed mistress." [328] But nonsense rhymes, the auricular absurdities of a Butler, Lowell, Carroll or Gilbert — faintly foreshadowed at least in Martial — and most other conscious drollery can hardly be dissevered from " phrasing." Certain rhetorical devices both lend themselves to the whimsical, extravagant, grotesque manner in which nearly any subject may be treated, and also can almost establish that whimsicality, extravagance, grotesquerie, which almost in itself is often amusing.

The figurative, metaphorical phrase such as appears in the message conveyed by a friend to his neighbour, the billiard enthusiast, " You're wanted at 'ome, Charlie. Yer wife's

just presented yer with another rebate off yer
income-tax; " the contrast or comparison carried to the point of absurdity —

Elusive Ulysses, they say, got away
From the Sirens, gay bane of the seas,
   Who provided demise, in attractive disguise,
For all sailors — real heavenly sprees.
Now Sirens 'twas hard, it is true, to eschew,
If one list to the strange song they sung.
   But I'd just like to see your Ulysses get free
When old Canius starts wagging his tongue; [329]

the massing of amusing material; the series of
comic descents; the abuse of some familiar
quotation —

The fact that I asked you last night
   To come over this evening and dine,
Procillus, would seem to be due
   To that fifth or sixth bottle of wine.
To think it entirely arranged
   And make notes on my babble — it's, why,
It's a terrible way to behave.
   Oh, that " In vino veritas " lie! [330]

the parody; the mock heroic; the understate-
ment; the hyperbole — it is figures such as
these that usually attend and create, serve as

midwives and mothers of drollery, and Martial
knew them all.

As one example of his use of the mock
heroic, for instance, we might cite his description of the toga given him by Parthenius, the
emperor's favorite. Sublimely eloquent he
ranges over the Latin language, Roman geog-
raphy and Greek mythology in his panegyric
upon that noble garment. Then in the last two
lines he suddenly descends to earth and intimates to Parthenius that the toga needs another sort of complement:

And yet — ah me! How folks will laugh and think
*   it such a joke*
To see this regal toga on a man with such a
*   cloak!* [331]

As for his use of exaggeration — he rivals
Artemus Ward, Josh Billings, Mark Twain,
and that other famous American who declared
it to be so cold in the States that he had once
seen a sheep frozen as it jumped and hang
there in mid air, a mass of ice. " But the law
of gravitation wouldn't have allowed that."
" Oh, that was frozen, too." Thais [332] is so thin
that Flaccus, who professes to be able to see
her, must be able to see nothing at all; Cae-

cilianus' [333] warm baths would make excellent refrigerators; the barber Antiochus is so deadly that

To *his mother, on hearing him, Pentheus would run,*
  And Orpheus with Maenads seek rest;
Why, on feeling his steel, stern Prometheus would reel,
  Call his bird and uncover his breast; [334]

the gold bowl Paulus [335] sent him is less substantial than butterflies' wings, spiders' webs, bubbles, Fabulla's make-up; his multiplicity of useless precautions against friends at Rome who insist on kissing one is a hyperbolical riot which eventually ends:

Though you're fev'rish or weeping or washing your head,
  Though you yawn, belch, or swim they don't miss.
You will still be their prey. To escape, the one way
  Is to love only those you won't kiss. [336]

But his most grotesque piece of accumulated, acervated, agglomerated exaggeration is perhaps his description of the estate given him by Lupus:

THOUGH *you gave me a farm — so you called it,
at least,*
  In a somewhat rhetorical turn —
It is really so small that all its soil, all,
  Could be put in my window-box urn.

A grove of Diana, you told me, I think,
  Was a notable sight on the place.
Your statement was true, if that one stunted rue
  Only occupied rather more space.

The wing of a cricket would cover that farm,
  And an overfed ant with the gout
Could not find enough crops to busy his chops
  To last till the sun flickered out.

Moreover, that garden you bragged so about
  Is a rosebud all ready to droop,
And the lawn's yield of grass would hardly surpass
  Its produce of spikenard and soup.

A cucumber never has room to lie straight,
  And a snake must reside there in pieces.
*A grasshopper hopped just one day and then
stopped,*
  Starved to death, its poor stomach in creases.

A *mole is the sole agriculturist there,*
   And he barely has room to turn round;
Not *a mushroom can spread, or a flower wave its*
    head
   Sans trespass on other folks' ground.

An *undergrown mouse, when it gets at that farm,*
   Makes it look as though hit by the plague,
And *my whole crop of hay was carried away*
   By a swallow just out of the egg.

My *demi-Priapus, his larger parts shorn,*
   Is so cramped that he needs a new cut.
My *harvest is stored in a minikin gourd,*
   And my wine in the shell of a nut.

The *term that you used in describing your gift*
   Was a syllable short, I feel:
It *is not an " e — state," but an empt — y state*
   Which I gladly would swap for a meal.[337]

The extent of this quotation is a final warn-
ing that our last chapter should come to its
unwilling close. The reader has been surfeited
with witticisms long since — and yet long before illustrations of the scope and variety of
Martial's wit can suffice the writer. But even
in this hurried survey of the subjects and meth-

ods of our humorists we catch at least a
glimpse of nearly all of the more or less distinct
kinds of quip and crank to be found in the
world's joke-book; and if we could always have
taken space to corroborate statement by evidence, it should be apparent to the most enthu-
siastic modernist that — slightly to misquote
and misapply Emerson's slightly exaggerated
statement — " we run very fast, but here is
this horrible Martial at the end of the course,
still abreast of us. Our novelties we can find
in him. He has anticipated our latest sally."
If his wit has seemed heavy, his humour jour-
nalese, it is our versions' fault, not his. A Pope
or an Austin Dobson might have done full justice to those Latin lines so sparkling, so entertaining, and withal so polished. Less jauntily
than before we quote again that uncharitable
jibe at another translator who did his luckless
best:

> *You take a towering genius*
> *And make him seem Perrault.*

VI. CONCLUSION

THE epigram is commonly supposed to be a short poem ending with a "sting," a supposition due to the authority of Martial, most of whose epigrams are of this sort. Yet most of the epigrams of the *Greek Anthology,* very many of those of Martial, and very many of those of modern poets are not of this sort at all. Our definition must be much enlarged. But however much it be enlarged, in Martial we find examples of every type of epigram that has ever been composed, and the volume and variety of his work, its general quality, and frequent perfection make him certainly the greatest epigrammatist of all time. Hard and coarse though he more than occasionally is, he lived in a hard, licentious age and should not be too unsparingly condemned for license in a form of poetry traditionally licentious, or for hardness which his fine friendships and much of his nobler verse belie. It is Martial, the master of stinging epigram, the model of satirical epigrammatists throughout

Europe for hundreds of years, the ancient wit familiar with almost every form of modern jest, whose influence has been the most profound; but upon our modern verse of every kind, from epigram to epic, his influence has been felt in varying degree, nor have our poets been the only ones to feel it: memorials of him stand in many fields of modern literature. His legacy to us has been a large one, and not its least part is his picture, the most interesting, the most complete, the most trustworthy we have, of life in that ancient and eternal city in that first century of our Lord, a life that contained so much, so very much, that prefigures and lures and well may warn a twentieth century likewise readier to feast with Nero than to follow with St. Paul.

NOTES AND BIBLIOGRAPHY

NOTES

Epigrams are cited from W. M. Lindsay's edition, Oxford, 1903. The writer wishes here to thank the translators, and their publishers, whose versions he has used. Acknowledgment of such borrowing is made wherever it occurs. For all other versions the writer is responsible.

1. *Simonides:* Walter Headlam.
2. *Callimachus:* Dr. J. A. Symonds.
3. *Julianus:* Goldwin Smith. **4.** *Palladas:* A. J. Butler
5. *Benserade:* Dr. Johnson. **6.** Landor.
7. W. H. D. Rouse. **8.** W. H. D. Rouse. **9.** J. A. Pott.
10. Cowper. **11.** R. G. Macgregor. **12.** XII. 23.
13. A. Wootten. **14.** G. B. Grundy. **15.** XI. 223.
16. *Palladas:* H. Wellesley. **17.** *Unknown:* J. H. Merivale.
18. *Ammianus:* J. H. Merivale.
19. *Palladas* (?): R. G. Macgregor.
20. R. G. Macgregor. **21.** J. A. Symonds: IX. 482 has 28 lines.
22. V. 34: There is some doubt whether the Fronto and Flaccilla referred to were his parents.
23. IX. 73. **24.** III. 38. **25.** In 84 or 85 B.C.; later appended as Books XIII and XIV. **26.** Books I and II in 85 or 86; Book III in 87 or 88; Book IV in 88; Book V. in 89; Book VI in 90; Book VII in 92; Book VIII in 93; Book IX in 94; Book X (1st edition in 95, 2nd in 98); Book XI in 96; Book XII in 101 or 102.
27. I. 1. **28.** VII. 16. **29.** XII. 12. **30.** V. 66.
31. Cf. Rev. James Davies, "Epigrams," in *The Quarterly Review*, CXVII. 204–249 (1865); H. P. Dodd, *The Epigrammatists*, London, 1870, Introduction, p. XIX; W. C. A. Ker,

Martial (*Loeb Library*), London, 1919, Introduction, p. XV;
K. F. Smith, *Martial the Epigrammatist*, Baltimore, 1920,
pp. 14–15.

32. Preface of Bk. I, Smith, *ibid.*, p. 22.   **33.** IX. 52.

34. I. 39. **35.** X. 47; W. J. Courthope. **36.** X. 23: W.
J. Courthope.

37. J. W. Mackail, Latin Literature, London 1899, p. 194.
38. Preface to Bk. XII: Ker. **39.** Smith, *ibid.*, p. 19.
40. J. W. Mackail, *ibid.*, p. 195. **41.** V. 34: K. F. Smith.
42. X. 53: cf. VI. 70. 11.   **43.** VI. 29.   **44.** IX. 28.
45. I. 88: George Lamb.   **46.** IV. 60.   **47.** X. 63.
48. XI. 13.   **49.** IX. 76.   **50.** I. 42.
51. X. 61.   **52.** VI. 32.   **53.** VI. 85.
54. V. 74.   **55.** V. 69: Anon., 1695.
56. I. 13.   **57.** VIII. 38.   **58.** XI. 5.
59. XI.36.   **60.** V. 58: Cowley.
61. I. 15.   **62.** VII. 47.   **63.** VIII. 77.
64. IV. 54.   **65.** L. S. 14.   **66.** VIII. 15.
67. XII. 98.   **68.** XII. 34: Hay.
69. II. 68: cf. II. 53.   **70.** J. S. Strachey.
71. X. 23.   **72.** I. 25.   **73.** VI.70.
74. XI. 56.   **75.** XII. 80.   **76.** V. 20.
77. V. 42: Hay.   **78.** XII. 10.
79. VIII. 12: Fletcher.   **80.** IV. 21.
81. VIII. 15.   **82.** XIV. 210.
83. II. 90: Courthope.   **84.** X. 47.
85. I. 3.   **86.** IV. 86: cf. XIII. 1.
87. VI. 82. **88.** V. 80.   **89.** VII. 97. **90.** IV. 10.
91. VII. 63. **92.** X. 4.   **93.** X. 46.   **94.** I. 16.
95. VII. 90. **96.** VIII. 29. **97.** VIII. 55. **98.** X. 20.
99. X. 33: Hay.   **100.** XIII. 2.
101. V. 24: cf. IX. 57.   **102.** IX. 97: cf. VII. 10.
103. IX. 11.   **104.** II. 86.   **105.** XI. 90.
106. IV. 13.   **107.** X. 38.   **108.** VII. 89.
109. X. 13.   **110.** X. 32.   **111.** X. 48.
112. X. 48.   **113.** XI. 52.   **114.** XI. 52.
115. I. 39.   **116.** V. 37: cf. III. 65.
117. III. 65: cf. XI. 8.   **118.** V. 37: cf. IV. 42.
119. I. 57: Hay.   **120.** XI. 104.

121. V. 83. **122.** IV. 22. **123.** VIII. 68.
124. XII. 84. **125.** I. 71. **126.** VIII. 50.
127. XI. 4. **128.** XII. 6. **129.** XI. 5.
130. XII. 6. **131.** L. S. 31. **132.** VIII. 36.
133. VIII. 21. **134.** X. 72. **135.** L. S. 3.
136. L. S. 25*b*. **137.** III. 35. **138.** IV. 32; VI. 15; IV. 59.
139. III. 56. **140.** VII. 19. **140a.** XII. 57: Courthope.
141. III. 58. **142.** Cf. X. 30; I. 55; I. 49; IV. 57;
IV. 64; X. 51; IV. 55; X. 37; XII. 31.
143. X. 30. **144.** IV. 5. **145.** XI. 103. **146.** XII. 51.
147. IX. 28. **148.** Pref. to Bk. I. **149.** III. 8.
150. I. 68. **151.** II. 25. **152.** III. 53.
153. IX. 10. **154.** XII. 92. **155.** II. 38.
156. II. 7. **157.** II. 64. **158.** III. 79.
159. VII. 10. **160.** XII. 46. **161.** I. 32.
162. I. 97. **163.** IX. 68. **164.** X. 62.
165. VIII. 7. **166.** XII. 72. **166a.** VI. 19.
167. I. 47. **168.** VIII. 74. **169.** VI. 53.
170. II. 88. **171.** VI. 14. **172.** VIII. 20. **173.** III. 44.
174. V. 73. **174a.** XI. 93. **175.** III. 9.
176. XII. 94. **177.** VIII. 18. **178.** XII. 63.
179. II. 20. **180.** I. 53. **181.** I. 72. **182.** I. 38.
183. I. 91. **184.** II. 8. **185.** VI. 60. **186.** XI. 90.
187. X. 45. **188.** XIII. 2. **189.** IX. 81.
190. VIII. 69. **191.** VIII. 35. **192.** IV. 24.
193. XII. 88. **194.** V. 28: Hay. **195.** V. 51.
196. I. 86. **197.** XI. 37. **198.** II. 16.
199. IV. 39. **200.** VII. 73. **201.** III. 26.
202. I. 64. **203.** VIII. 48. **204.** X. 65.
205. XII. 39. **206.** III. 63. **207.** I. 9.
208. XII. 16. **209.** VIII. 10. **210.** II. 74.
211. VII. 70. **212.** XII. 17. **213.** III. 10.
214. VII. 98. **215.** I. 28. **216.** I. 87. **217.** XII. 12.
218. II. 80. **219.** II. 26. **220.** XII. 56. **221.** IV. 56.
222. VI. 63. **223.** XII. 40: cf. VIII. 27. **224.** XI. 67.
225. X. 97. **226.** II. 65. **227.** V. 37. **228.** X. 43.
229. X. 8. **230.** VII. 39. **231.** II. 89. **232.** IX. 47.
233. IX. 27. **234.** II. 36. **235.** XII. 70.
236. I. 33. **237.** I. 75. **238.** III. 52.

239. XI. 66. **240.** XII. 54. **241.** VI. 72.

242. VIII. 43. **243.** III. 37: cf. XII. 13.

244. VII. 43. **245.** II. 44. **246.** I. 98.

247. V. 52. **248.** II. 24. **249.** IX. 46. **250.** I. 103.

251. I. 99. **252.** VIII. 6. **253.** VII. 48.

254. III. 60. **255.** XII. 50. **256.** VIII. 14.

257. III. 45: cf. III. 50. **258.** V. 81. **259.** XII. 87.

260. V. 76. **261.** VIII. 19. **262.** III. 30.

263. XI. 34. **264.** II. 11. **265.** XII. 82.

266. IX. 14. **267.** VII. 76. **268.** IX. 35.

269. III. 32. **270.** I. 100. **271.** X. 39. **272.** II. 21.

273. I. 83. **274.** II. 41. **275.** VI. 74. **276.** I. 19.

277. V. 49. **278.** VI. 57. **279.** III. 43. **280.** VI. 12.

281. III. 93. **282.** IX. 37. **283.** III. 57. **284.** VII. 83.

285. With apologies to Horace and Austin Dobson.

286. IV. 65. **287.** VIII. 60. **288.** IX. 98. **289.** IX. 78.

290. II. 52. **291.** V. 35. **292.** X. 79.

293. VIII. 17. **294.** V. 4. **295.** VIII. 9.

296. XI. 76. **297.** IX. 102. **298.** I. 85.

299. XII. 7. **299a.** VII. 4. **299b.** IV. 69.

300. IX. 62. **301.** XII. 26. **302.** V. 21.

303. II. 10. **304.** IX. 29. **305.** X. 36. **306.** III. 29.

307. IX. 96. **308.** VII. 54. **309.** VIII. 40. **310.** V. 75.

311. III. 94. **312.** X. 16. **313.** XI. 107. **314.** III. 61.

315. IV. 43. **316.** V. 47. **317.** III. 41. **318.** III. 55.

319. IV. 41. **320.** II. 77. **321.** II. 12. 5.

322. I. 10. **323.** VIII. 13. **324.** VIII. 59.

325. VII. 38. **326.** VIII. 23. **327.** I. 11.

328. XI. 73. **329.** III. 64. **330.** I. 27. **331.** VIII. 28.

332. XI. 101. **333.** II. 78. **334.** XI. 84.

335. VIII. 33. **336.** XI. 98. **337.** XI. 18.

BIBLIOGRAPHY

AMOS, A., *Martial and the Moderns*. Cambridge, 1858.

BOISSIER, G., *Tacitus and Other Roman Studies*. Translated by W. G. Hutchison. (*Cf.* Chapter: *The Poet Martial*) London and New York, 1906.

BRIGGS, W. D., " Source Material for Jonson's *Epigrams* and *Forest*," in *Classical Philology*, XI. 169–190 (1916).

BUTLER, H. E., *Post-Augustan Poetry*. Oxford, 1909.

COURTHOPE, W. J., *Selections from Martial* (Translated or Imitated in English Verse). London, 1914.

CRAIG, V. J., *Martial's Wit and Humor* (University of Pennsylvania Dissertation). Philadelphia, 1912.

DODD, H. P., *The Epigrammatists*. London, 1870.

FRIEDLAENDER, L., *M. Valerii Martialis Epigrammaton Libri* mit erklärenden Anmerkungen. 2 vols. Leipzig, 1886.

GRUNDY, G. B., *Ancient Gems in Modern Settings*. Oxford, 1913.

KER, W. C. A., *Martial, with an English Translation*, in *The Loeb Classical Library*. 2 vols. London and New York, 1919, 1920.

LESSING, G. E., *Anmerkungen über das Epigramm*. Berlin, 1771.

LEVY, R., *Martial und die deutsche Epigrammatik des siebzehnten Jahrhunderts*. Stuttgart, 1903.

LINDSAY, W. M., *The Ancient Editions of Martial*. Oxford, 1903.

McDANIEL, W. B., " Martial, His Fools and Rogues," in *University of Pennsylvania Lectures*, V. 405–431 (1918).

NIXON, P., *A Roman Wit*. Boston, 1911.

" Herrick and Martial," in *Classical Philology*, V. 189–202 (1910).

POST, E., *Selected Epigrams of Martial*. Boston, 1908.

BIBLIOGRAPHY

POTT and WRIGHT, *Martial, The Twelve Books of Epigrams*
(Translated by J. A. Pott and F. A. Wright). London
and New York, 1925.

SCHNEIDEWIN, F. G., *M. Valerii Martialis Epigrammaton
Libri.* 2 vols. Grimma, 1842. Leipzig, 1853.

SMITH, K. F., *Martial the Epigrammatist*. Baltimore, 1920.

INDEX OF EPIGRAMS OF MARTIAL

[205]

INDEX OF EPIGRAMS

INDEX OF EPIGRAMS

INDEX OF EPIGRAMS

Our Debt to Greece and Rome

AUTHORS AND TITLES

AUTHORS AND TITLES

Homer. *John A. Scott.*

Sappho. *David M. Robinson.*

Euripides. *F. L. Lucas.*

Aristophanes. *Louis E. Lord.*

Demosthenes. *Charles D. Adams.*

The Poetics of Aristotle. *Lane Cooper.*

Greek Rhetoric and Literary Criticism. *W. Rhys Roberts.*

Lucian. *Francis G. Allinson.*

Cicero and His Influence. *John C. Rolfe.*

Catullus. *Karl P. Harrington.*

Lucretius and His Influence. *George Depue Hadzsits.*

Ovid. *Edward Kennard Rand.*

Horace. *Grant Showerman.*

Virgil. *John William Mackail.*

Seneca the Philosopher. *Richard Mott Gummere.*

Apuleius. *Elizabeth Hazelton Haight.*

Martial. *Paul Nixon.*

Platonism. *Alfred Edward Taylor.*

Aristotelianism. *John L. Stocks.*

Stoicism. *Robert Mark Wenley.*

Language and Philology. *Roland G. Kent.*

AUTHORS AND TITLES